DIVORCE GUIDE FOR ONTARIO

DIVORCE GUIDE FOR ONTARIO
Step-by-step guide for obtaining your own divorce

Sandra J. Meyrick, M.Sc., LL.B.

Self-Counsel Press
(a division of)
International Self-Counsel Press Ltd.
Canada U.S.A.

Printed in Canada

First edition: May 1973
Tenth edition: April 1993
Eleventh edition: April 1994
Twelfth edition: May 1995
Thirteenth edition: June 1996
Fourteenth edition: April 1997

Canadian Cataloguing in Publication Data

Meyrick, Sandra J.
    Divorce guide for Ontario

    (Self-counsel legal series)
    First-2nd eds. by Ronald J. Reid; 3rd-5th eds. by J.D. James; 6th-10th eds.
by Gloria J. Epstein; 1st ed. published in 1983 under title: Ontario divorce guide; 2nd ed.
published under title: Divorce guide for Ontario: how to obtain your own divorce.

    ISBN 1-55180-109-4

    1. Divorce — Law and legislation — Ontario — Popular works. 2. Divorce —
Law and legislation — Ontario — Forms. I. Title. II. Series.
KEO224.Z82E67 1997   346.71301'66   C97-910102-6
KF535.Z9E67 1997

Self-Counsel Press
(a division of)
International Self-Counsel Press Ltd.

1481 Charlotte Road   1704 N. State Street
North Vancouver, British Columbia V7J 1H1   Bellingham, Washington 98225

CONTENTS

TABLES

SAMPLES

NOTICE TO READERS

SERVICES AVAILABLE FROM THE PUBLISHER

To obtain your divorce, you will have to file certain forms with the divorce court. You may type all of these forms yourself, but it is easier and quicker to fill in pre-printed forms. The use of pre-printed forms is common in the legal profession as it eases the typing load considerably.

Self-Counsel Press stocks two sets of forms suitable for use in most cases: one set if you are filing for divorce as a sole petitioner and one set if you and your spouse are filing as joint petitioners. **Note:** If you and/or your spouse live in Hamilton, London, Barrie, Kingston, and/or Napanee and plan to file an uncontested divorce in Ontario Court (General Division) Family Court, formerly the Unified Family Court, you need different forms. Please see the section in the book referring to this procedure. If you are in the Family Court System, you should be able to get the necessary forms, free of charge, from the courthouse.

MAKE SURE YOU HAVE THE CORRECT SET OF FORMS BEFORE OPENING THE KIT. Please read this book for further information about which set of forms you need. When you fill out these forms, read them carefully and complete them by following the instructions and samples in this book.

1. Divorce Forms for Ontario (Sole Petitioner) $16.95

Contains —

2 Petitions for Divorce
1 Financial Statement
1 Net Family Property Statement
2 Notices to File Financial Statement
2 Acknowledgment of Receipt cards
2 Affidavits of Service
2 Affidavits of Service (by mail)
2 Requisitions/Notice of Motion
2 Petitioner's Affidavits
2 Divorce Judgments
2 Certificates of Divorce
2 Requisitions
2 Affidavits (re no appeal)
2 Support Deduction Orders
2 Support Deduction Information Forms
2 Case Information Statements

2. Joint Divorce Forms for Ontario (Joint Petitioners) $16.95

Contains —

2 Joint Petitions for Divorce
2 Notices of Motion
2 Joint Affidavits
2 Financial Statements
2 Waivers of Financial Statements
2 Divorce Judgments
2 Certificates of Divorce
2 Support Deduction Orders
2 Requisitions
2 Affidavits (re no appeal)
2 Support Deduction Information Forms
2 Case Information Statements

To obtain any of these packages of pre-printed forms, complete the following order form and mail it with your money order or MasterCard or Visa number, or purchase them where you bought this book.

(Prices subject to change without notice.)

✄ . . . .

ORDER FORM

TO: Self-Counsel Press
4 Bram Court
Brampton, ON L6W 3R6

Enclosed is a money order for $ _____ which is payment in full for:

_____   set(s) of Divorce Forms for Ontario (Sole Petitioner) at
              $16.95 each   _____

_____   set(s) of Divorce Forms for Ontario (Joint Petitioners) at
              $16.95 each   _____

              plus $3.00 postage and handling   _____

              Subtotal   _____

              Add 7% GST to subtotal   _____

              Add 8% PST to subtotal   _____

              TOTAL: _____

Name: _____

Address: _____

City: _____

Province: _____ Postal code: _____

Telephone: _____

MasterCard/Visa number:_____

Expiration date: _____ Validation date: _____

Signature: _____

1
CAN I DO MY OWN DIVORCE?

a. DO I NEED A LAWYER?

Although the philosophy of this publication is self-help, there are cases in which you *cannot* handle the divorce yourself and will require professional advice or assistance. Specifically, if your divorce will be contested by your spouse, you should not attempt to handle it without the services of a lawyer. This publication is intended to help you decide whether or not your case is one in which the assistance of a lawyer is necessary and then how to process your divorce effectively.

Even if your divorce is uncontested, there may be procedural complications that will require the services of a lawyer. For example, if you have no idea where your spouse is living, you may have trouble serving the Petition for Divorce on him or her.

There may also be maintenance payments to be negotiated or, perhaps, problems of proof in certain circumstances. If you require special advice, you can retain the services of a lawyer for limited purposes only, while you complete the bulk of the work yourself.

In some cases, no court appearance will be necessary. However, if your case is one in which a court attendance is required, you should consider retaining a lawyer to handle the actual hearing in court. For approximately $600, most divorce lawyers will read your documents, take the case into court, and file the Divorce Judgment (i.e., the judge's order for divorce). You are, of course, entitled to represent yourself in court in any action. The choice is yours.

If, however, you do elect to retain a lawyer to handle your court case, you should do the following:

(a) Be sure to choose a lawyer who carries on a matrimonial practice.

(b) Ask for a quotation beforehand (this applies to any legal service).

(c) Make sure your lawyer agrees to handle only those parts of the procedure with which you are not comfortable.

If you decide to handle your divorce yourself, remember that even with the recent changes to the law and rules, obtaining your own divorce still requires a good measure of intelligence, perseverance, and concentration.

b. THINK BEFORE YOU START

Think twice about everything you are doing. Be fully aware of all the consequences but particularly what the position of you, your spouse, and your children will be as a result of your decision to bring a divorce action. Seek help from a marriage counsellor or other qualified person if you feel there is any chance of reconciliation.

If you are determined to proceed with a divorce, you may wish to pursue mediation. In any event, follow all the suggested procedures very carefully; they are all important. Likewise, all forms must be completed with meticulous attention to detail. If you do sloppy work, you could end up paying a lawyer twice as much to correct your mistakes. Be methodical and well prepared at all times.

Be persistent. Don't be afraid to ask questions about the law, even though there may be people who try to discourage your inquiries. Your sincerity and politeness will encourage the proper responses. Contrary to what you might have heard, the divorce courts are quite efficient. Let's keep them that way by not clogging the process with defective papers and pleadings.

If you must appear in court and you intend to represent yourself, you must be especially well prepared. The judge is not there to block your efforts to obtain a divorce. However, the judge does have a specific job to do and must be satisfied that the requirements of the Divorce Act have been complied with. This book provides an outline of the types of questions that will be asked. However, you should make a point of attending at least one court session of uncontested divorces in order to familiarize yourself with the conduct of a divorce trial.

If you find yourself getting in over your head, you will have to make a decision —

(a) to consult a lawyer, or

(b) to drop the action.

The choice is entirely a personal one but, in any event, don't proceed if you do not have a clear understanding of what you are doing. The consequences of errors can be serious and permanent.

c. HOW CAN THIS BOOK HELP ME?

This book is divided into two basic parts. The first part outlines the existing law concerning a divorce action. It discusses the various grounds on which you may proceed. The second part deals with the step-by-step procedure leading to the securing of the Divorce Judgment.

There are various objective tests to meet before you have the right to a divorce. A copy of the Divorce Act is provided in Appendix 4 for your information. Make sure you understand the grounds under which you are proceeding and that you satisfy the requirements of the particular section you are using. You cannot immediately obtain a divorce just because you and your spouse have agreed to break up.

Marriage breakdown is the sole ground for divorce. There are, however, limitations on the means of proving marriage breakdown. There are three different ways you can declare marriage breakdown: one-year separation, adultery, or cruelty. If you have lived apart for less than one year you must either wait until one year has passed before the divorce can be granted or establish your case based on adultery or cruelty.

You do not have to wait that long if your spouse has left and you wish to collect support, if custody of children must be determined, or if you want an early division of matrimonial property. If you wish, these areas of relief can be pursued separately under the Family Law Act, which is provincial legislation. This book does not cover these remedies, and if you decide that any of these remedies offers the most appropriate form of relief for you, you will have to see a lawyer, legal aid office, or family court official. You might also refer to the Ontario edition of *Marriage, Separation, and Divorce*, another title in the Self-Counsel Series.

It is important to recognize that the problems of proof vary according to the section of the act you use as the basis of your divorce. Obviously, it will be easy for you to start your divorce, all things being equal, under a section that sets out simple and straightforward grounds. But, if you run into any serious difficulties in preparing your Petition, or any serious problems of proof, it will be necessary for you to consult a lawyer to put you back on the proper course.

If you feel that there are two or more sections of the Divorce Act you can use to plead marriage breakdown, you should use them all as your chances of success will increase accordingly.

The second part of the book is where you will find step-by-step procedures. Directions are given for starting your action and all the stages up to the completed divorce. The procedure is the same throughout the province except in Hamilton, London, Barrie, Kingston, and Napanee. (See chapter 6 if you live in these areas.)

Your divorce will be heard in the region where either you or your spouse is living. The local registrar's office where you begin your action is located in the regional courthouse.

Each step outlined in this book is important, and each one must be completed before you proceed to the next. Failure to do so will only result in a great deal of delay and confusion at a later stage.

Do not allow technical words to confuse you. If you encounter terms or phrases foreign to you, look them up in a legal dictionary, which can be found at any library, or consult another professional source. A glossary of the most common terms is provided at the back of this book for your use. Keep a notebook of such information. It will pay you to research your divorce carefully. Again, it is emphasized that ignorance in the early stages can "snowball" into later difficulties.

This book also shows all the forms you will need and illustrates how they should be completed. These are included as samples only of commonly used sentences and phrases. If your specific situation does not fit these examples, do not copy from the forms, just use them as guides to the general style and form required.

It is not difficult to draft your own clauses. Put a little work into writing properly structured sentences and, generally, if they state the truth, they will be accepted.

While you are following the step-by-step procedure, you will find it necessary to refer constantly to these forms. You may not see the reason for some of them, but they are all necessary for the successful completion of your action.

d. SUMMARY

The following is a list of circumstances that must apply to you if you want to process your own divorce:

(a) You can prove marriage breakdown in a straightforward way (see chapter 2).

(b) You can serve your spouse without undue difficulty (i.e., your spouse lives in Canada and isn't avoiding service of the documents).

(c) There are no contentious issues between you and your spouse in areas such as custody of and access to the children or support for you and/or the children.

(d) You are not advancing a claim to property that is being opposed by your spouse.

2
GROUNDS FOR DIVORCE

Under the Divorce Act, there is only one ground for divorce. The Divorce Act, in subsection 8(1), establishes marriage breakdown as the sole criterion for divorce. However, subsection 8(2) does limit the ways you can prove a marriage breakdown. Marriage breakdown can be established in these cases:

(a) If you and your spouse have lived separately for at least one year before the Divorce Judgment (although you may begin the paperwork any time after your separation begins)

(b) If the spouse against whom a divorce is sought has committed adultery or has treated you with physical or mental cruelty of such a kind as to make it intolerable for the two of you to live together.

a. ONE-YEAR SEPARATION (Section 8(2)(a))

Under section 8(2)(a) of the Divorce Act, the period during which you and your spouse must have been separated to qualify for a divorce is one year, and either you or your spouse may commence proceedings without waiting until that period has expired. All that is necessary is that you and your spouse be separated at the time the proceedings are started. The one-year period of separation will be satisfied provided that 12 months have elapsed before the Divorce Judgment is granted.

It is important to note that the period of separation must be uninterrupted up to the time the Divorce Judgment is granted. However, the Divorce Act does make provisions for efforts to reconcile. You and your spouse may live together after separation without eliminating the accumulation of time toward the one-year period as long as each temporary period or periods of living together do not exceed 90 days in total. When determining whether you and your spouse have been separated for one year, any and all total periods of attempted reconciliation lasting 90 days or less will be included. This is the case even though there may, in addition, have been casual acts of sexual intercourse.

For example, if you and your spouse were living apart for ten months, then resumed cohabitation for more than 90 days, and then separated again, the first ten months could not be used to establish a period of separation. In this case, you would have to begin calculating your period of separation at the start of your second separation.

It does not matter whether the separation has occurred by consent of the spouses or by seemingly totally unjustified "desertion" by one spouse. In the event of a unilateral separation, either spouse or both can commence divorce proceedings.

Often people are confused about what separation means and when it starts. If one spouse leaves the matrimonial home, that is usually a clear sign of the commencement of separation. However, spouses may have been living "separate and apart" and remain in the same dwelling as long as they have been living independent lives.

Finally, it is significant that *both* spouses may apply for divorce when the ground is marriage breakdown based on a one-year separation. You cannot obtain a divorce on the basis of your own adultery (nor can your spouse on the ground of his or her own adultery).

b. ADULTERY (Section 8(2)(b)(i))

Under the Divorce Act, marriage breakdown can also be established if you can prove that your spouse has committed adultery.

You do not have to name the person with whom your spouse has allegedly committed adultery. However, if you decide to name the person as a co-respondent (your spouse would be the other respondent), then you must serve that person with a copy of the Petition. The only case in which it is necessary to name the third party is when you are making a claim against that party.

The situation may arise where you know that your spouse has committed adultery and you want to assert a specific claim against that person but you do not know the name of the other person involved. You can, in these circumstances, simply serve your spouse with the Petition for Divorce and then, when you later find out the name of the person with whom the adultery was committed, amend your Petition and serve the document on the other party to the proceeding.

It is not necessary for you to find your spouse in bed with another person to corroborate your own evidence of your spouse's adultery. You need only establish the probability that such adultery occurred. Circumstantial evidence such as a mutual friend seeing men's and women's clothing in the bedroom closet after you have already separated from your spouse is usually enough to establish adultery.

If your spouse has an illegitimate child, obtain a copy of the birth certificate from the Registrar General, P.O. Box 4600, Thunder Bay, Ontario, P7B 6L8 if the birth was in Ontario, and use the certificate to corroborate your evidence of adultery. Refer to Appendix 2 for a list of Vital Statistics Departments in the various provinces to write to for information.

Send a money order with your request. The amount will vary according to the province. The payee differs by province — for instance, in Ontario the money order should be made payable to the Minister of Finance; in Alberta the payee is the Provincial Treasurer — you might wish to leave the payee space blank.

If your only corroboration is a birth certificate, you may run into difficulties, as a judge may be hesitant to accept the illegitimacy of a child. In this case, I recommend that you do not proceed unless your spouse is prepared to admit the alleged adultery under oath (i.e., orally at trial or in an affidavit or an examination for discovery as will be described later), or there is an independent witness available to testify. A private detective can be hired to obtain the evidence or, if you are short of funds, you can ask a friend. One drawback of using a friend is that he or she may be reluctant to become involved. The best and cheapest witness is one not connected to either party, such as a landlord or a next-door neighbor.

1. By affidavit evidence

The simplest way to obtain a divorce on the grounds of marriage breakdown based on adultery is by the affidavit evidence of your spouse and, preferably, by the person with whom your spouse is alleged to have committed adultery. The affidavit of your spouse should state that he or she understands that there is no obligation to provide the evidence given. Your spouse should also say that he or she has received a copy of the Petition for Divorce and has reviewed the facts alleged with respect to adultery and that these facts are correct. Alternatively, any corrections to those facts should be indicated. Your spouse should also confirm the date you separated and that the adultery has not been condoned. Further, it should be stated that there is no possibility of reconciliation.

If possible, an affidavit from the person with whom your spouse is alleged to have committed adultery should also be filed with the court. The affidavit should state that this person is not obliged to give evidence of adultery, but has reviewed the facts alleged in the Petition with respect to adultery and that the facts are correct or, again, any corrections required should be indicated.

Alternatively, an affidavit can be filed by someone who is in a position to confirm the adultery alleged against your spouse. For example, a friend may be able to provide the evidence proving that your spouse is living common-law.

2. By examination for discovery

Adultery can also be proved to the court by filing a transcript of an examination for discovery. This is the process you would use if you feel that a court appearance will be necessary to settle certain contested matters, but your spouse, although prepared to admit to the allegation of adultery, is unwilling or unable to attend court. In this instance, you may want to hire a lawyer who practises in the city or town where your spouse lives to conduct the examination for discovery. Your spouse, if he or she is co-operative, can call around to find out the fees of lawyers in the area for this service and forward the information to you so that you can hire the lawyer of your choice. Otherwise your nearest large library will have books with lists of names of lawyers who practise in different areas.

The lawyer will make an appointment to meet with a court reporter and your spouse. The court reporter will put your spouse under oath, just as a judge would if your spouse appeared in court. The lawyer will then ask the questions that will show on the transcript of the examination for discovery that your spouse is the proper respondent to the action and that the acts of adultery complained of in the Petition are admitted to. The court reporter will take down all of the questions and answers. In order to have as strong corroborative evidence as possible, a similar examination of the person with whom the adultery is alleged to have been committed is advisable. Arrangements can usually be made to have the two examinations proceed one after the other.

The question and answer period usually takes less than half an hour, even if two people are being examined. In a few weeks, you will receive a copy of the questions and answers. The cost of hiring a lawyer to do this should range from $300 to $500 plus the cost of the court reporter and the transcript of the examination for discovery.

Once you receive the transcript you can make a photocopy for yourself; if a court appearance is still necessary you should take the transcript to court with you and hand the original to the clerk. When the judge requests evidence of the grounds on which the divorce is proceeding, the transcript of the examination for discovery will be marked as an exhibit.

Alternatively, it may appear, after the examination for discovery, that the divorce can proceed without a court appearance. In this instance you can file the transcripts instead of the affidavits.

The judge will read over the transcript either privately or in court to make sure that the proper party was served and that he or she made the admissions under oath. If you are in court, the judge will then proceed with questions on the rest of the Petition. You will be asked few, if any, questions about the grounds for divorce.

3. By court appearance

Finally, adultery can be proved by your appearance and testimony in court, preferably with your spouse who is prepared to corroborate the adultery. If your spouse is unwilling or unable to come to court to corroborate and you do not have transcripts of an examination for discovery, then you may be able to have the adultery corroborated through the testimony of a person with whom adultery is alleged to have been committed or through the testimony of an independent third person. In a court appearance as well, the filing of the birth certificate of a child of your spouse and another person would be helpful.

As you can appreciate, the court must be entirely satisfied that your spouse is being truthful in this type of situation before a divorce will be granted. Your spouse's evidence, whether through an affidavit, examination for discovery, or appearance in court, *must* be voluntary, and there must be no suggestion that you and your spouse have entered into an agreement to fabricate evidence.

Therefore, as a safeguard, it is essential that you do not enter into an agreement with your spouse that he or she will provide evidence in court until after you have commenced divorce proceedings and have had all the necessary documents served. This will indicate that admissions made by your spouse under oath are admissions of fact as set out in your Petition and that there was no fabrication of evidence. (When you allege that "there has been no collusion" in your Petition for Divorce, you are stating that no evidence has been fabricated, nor have you and your spouse joined together to "create" evidence.)

4. Summary

In conclusion, if you intend to obtain your own divorce on the grounds of your spouse's adultery, you must be able to provide independent proof that the adultery you are alleging actually took place. A written letter of confession from your spouse is not sufficient. One of the following types of proof is required.

(a) Where a court appearance is not necessary you may file —

   (i) an affidavit sworn by your spouse confirming the particulars of the alleged adultery,

   (ii) an affidavit sworn by the person who is alleged to have committed the adultery with your spouse, again confirming the particulars of the adultery,

   (iii) transcripts of the examinations for discovery of the spouse and the person with whom the adultery is alleged, or

   (iv) an affidavit from a person or persons in a position to confirm the adultery.

(b) Where a court appearance is necessary, you may —

   (i) call your spouse as the witness to the adultery complained of if he or she is willing to come to court and admit to the adultery alleged in your Petition,

   (ii) call as a witness the person with whom your spouse is alleged to have committed adultery if he or she is willing to come to court and admit to the adultery alleged,

   (iii) use transcripts from an examination for discovery,

   (iv) call a witness who has seen your spouse living with the other person as husband and wife, or

   (v) call a witness who has seen the other person stay overnight on various occasions at your spouse's residence.

It would be inadvisable for you to attempt to obtain your own divorce on the grounds of marriage breakdown based on adultery unless you can provide the court with suitable evidence as outlined above. If none of these procedures is available to you, you must consult a lawyer.

c. CRUELTY (Section 8(2)(b)(ii))

Breakdown of the marriage may be established if your spouse has treated you with physical or mental cruelty of such a kind as to make continued cohabitation intolerable.

It is impossible to describe all types of contact that may constitute cruelty or those falling short of cruelty. The courts have not tried to define cruelty. However, an ordinary understanding may signify the disposition to inflict suffering, to delight in or exhibit indifference to your misery, or to demonstrate hard-heartedness. If, in your marriage relationship, your spouse causes unnecessary pain to your body or emotions, his or her conduct may constitute cruelty that will entitle you to dissolution of a marriage if such actions render your cohabitation intolerable.

If you decide to proceed under this section, you must be able to establish that the cruelty is of grave nature and not merely conduct that can be characterized as incompatibility of personalities. The whole matrimonial relationship must be considered, especially if the cruelty consists of complaints, accusations, or what may be called nagging.

The courts will want to consider what effect the allegedly cruel conduct has had

on you. In the final analysis, determination of what constitutes cruelty must depend on the circumstances of each case while considering the personal characteristics of you and your spouse and your attitude toward the marriage relationship.

To demonstrate a marriage breakdown based on cruelty you must, therefore, specify the conduct on the part of your spouse that makes living together intolerable, provide as accurately as possible the times and places of the cruelty, and have a witness who can corroborate the conduct complained of and its effect on you. The evidence of a physician, psychiatrist, or other professional person is invaluable.

In many cases there may be no other person who knows of your spouse's cruelty. You may still proceed with your Petition; however, your evidence must be very strong to obtain a divorce without corroborating evidence. It is very important to give an accurate and detailed account in both your Petition and your evidence of the cruel conduct of your spouse and the effects on you of such conduct.

As with the other manifestations of marriage breakdown, you can proceed either by way of affidavit evidence or by a court appearance. If you use an affidavit, you must file one that indicates the relationship of the person swearing the affidavit to you (e.g., a friend, relative, employer, doctor) and gives details of any acts of cruelty or evidence of cruelty witnessed by the person. Alternatively, a copy of a medical report signed by a medical practitioner licensed to practice in Ontario may be attached as an exhibit to your affidavit.

3
ADDITIONAL MATTERS

a. CUSTODY

Both natural parents of the child have equal rights to custody. This situation remains until a court makes an order to the contrary or until the parents enter into a written agreement giving sole custody, care, and control of the children to either the mother or the father, or agreeing to a joint custody arrangement.

It used to be that in most cases the mother had custody of the children, particularly when they were very young. But times have changed, and in an increasing number of cases, custody is being granted to the father. There are, as well, an increasing number of situations where the parents agree to co-operate in the joint upbringing of their children. In these cases a joint custody arrangement is entered into in which all the major decisions pertaining to the children are shared by the parents even though care and control may predominately be with one parent or split between both parents.

If a custody agreement cannot be reached, the issue must be heard by a judge. In any contested hearing before the court, the judge is concerned with one matter only: the best interests of the children.

If there is any suggestion whatsoever that there is to be a contested custody hearing, you must consult a lawyer. However, it may be that you wish to obtain an uncontested divorce and leave the issue of custody and support to another hearing. In this case, you can proceed and obtain a divorce on your own and then start a corollary relief action for a decision pertaining only to custody and support. If you decide to go this route, it would be wise to consult a lawyer beforehand, as certain of your rights, particularly those of property, may be affected. The division of property is not discussed in detail in this book as it falls under provincial legislation called the Family Law Act, which is not covered here. Also, it is important to retain a lawyer for the corollary relief action as it is complicated and generally requires a court appearance.

Once a court order is made awarding either the husband or the wife custody, the issue is not necessarily final. The spouse who does not have custody or day-to-day care and control of the children can, at a later date, if circumstances have changed considerably, apply to the court to have the issue of custody reviewed. If satisfied that a change in custody would be in the best interests of the child or children, the judge can vary the original custody order whether or not it was obtained on consent.

You should note that the Divorce Act expressly empowers the court to order joint or shared parenting privileges between spouses, although it falls short of endorsing any presumption in favor of joint custody. There are decisions from Ontario courts that support joint custody and others that do not. It is clear that the trend is to support joint custody arrangements, especially where the parents are able to co-operate. In Ontario, some courts have ordered alternating monthly custody arrangements in a joint custody situation notwithstanding that each parent had sought an order for sole custody.

Under the Divorce Act, the court may grant joint custody to the spouse or to one or both of the spouses and any other person such as a close relative. You should keep in mind that orders allowing custody and/or access to third parties will not be made unless that person consents and an opportunity has been given to the court to assess the qualifications of the third party to enjoy custodial or access privileges.

According to the Divorce Act, the courts must apply the principle that a child of the marriage should have as much contact with each parent as is consistent with the best interests of the child. For that purpose the court shall take into consideration the willingness of the person for whom custody is sought to facilitate such contact.

These provisions were intended to encourage maximum access between the child and the non-custodial parent. If one spouse is prepared to facilitate maximum contact between the child and the other spouse, whereas the other spouse is opposed to allowing generous access privileges and both spouses are equally competent parents, then the court should grant sole custody to the spouse who will promote maximum contact provided that this is consistent with the best interests of the child.

The act also gives broad discretion to the court to make custody or access orders for specified periods and subject to other terms or conditions. The court has the express authority to grant a temporary or fixed-term order for custody or access, which may be reviewed at a later date. In other words, in some circumstances, the court could order an independent assessment of the family to try to determine the needs of the child and the ability of the respective parents to fulfill those needs. Alternatively, the court could refer the parties to a mediator who might assist in working out custody and access arrangements.

You should keep in mind that it is rare for the courts to grant custody orders for children over the age of 16 years.

It is most unusual for a spouse not having custody of the children to be deprived of the right to see them. The judge is more likely to consider it in the best interests of the children to have a relationship with both parents. As has been said earlier, if you interfere with your spouse's access to the children, you stand the chance of losing custody as, all else being equal, a court is going to be inclined to award custody to the spouse who will provide the greatest opportunity for access.

The courts also often prefer the parents to work out their own arrangements for access and will grant an order for "reasonable," "liberal," or "generous" access. Such an order provides the flexibility to accommodate the interests of the parents and the children.

If the parents are unable to work out the terms of access themselves, the court will fix appropriate times and places if necessary. The court may also impose additional restrictions such as limiting the custodial parent's right to take the children out of the jurisdiction or directing that access privileges be exercised under the supervision of a third party if the non-custodial parent has abused his or her access privileges.

b. FINANCIAL RELIEF

1. In general

Read the provisions of sections 15 to 19 of the Divorce Act (see Appendix 4). These sections regulate the jurisdiction of the court to order relief in terms of support for you and/or the children, custody, and access.

An original application for temporary or permanent support for you or the child or children of the marriage may be made by either or both spouses or former spouses. Apparently, a joint application is possible. There is no longer a distinction between payments made before divorce and after. Accordingly, the terms "alimony" and "maintenance" have been replaced by the term "support."

Neither party to a divorce action is automatically entitled to spousal support. The court will look at any fact it feels is relevant to a person's request for support. The court will likely consider the "needs" of the party seeking support and the "means" or ability to pay of the other spouse (the "payor" spouse). Detailed statements of finances and property must be submitted by both spouses to allow a court to determine whether support is appropriate.

A husband may be able to secure support on his own behalf from his wife or, as is more often the case, the wife from the husband. A support order can be for a fixed period of time within which the wife is expected to rehabilitate herself and put herself in a position where she is self-supporting.

The judge will be concerned with factors such as the earnings of both parties, the ability of the spouse seeking support to hold a job or to secure employment, his or her education level, training, health, and other related matters.

The judge can order either the husband or the wife to make monthly payments in an amount specified by the judge and/or a lump sum settlement instead of support payments.

Sometimes, if the petitioner successfully obtains an order for support, the judge will not specify an amount at the time of the hearing, but will refer the matter to a family court judge, or to a family law reference for the determination of the proper sum to be paid. The petitioner must then appear before the court officer who will hear all necessary evidence regarding respective incomes and expenses of the spouses and will then arrive at the amount of support payments to be made. If your spouse is working and living in the province, you should retain the services of a lawyer to conduct the hearing on your behalf. However, if your spouse is not employed or his

or her actual whereabouts are not known, you are probably wasting your time and money trying to collect support.

Many people do not realize that they can often use the facilities of family courts in Ontario to obtain an order requiring their spouses to make support payments on their behalf and/or on behalf of the children of the marriage. If you are unsure whether or not you wish to start divorce proceedings, but you do require support, you should contact the family court officials in your district. They will advise you of your rights and will help you exercise those rights as quickly as possible. You do not require a lawyer and should have no difficulty presenting your case.

Your children have a right to support that cannot be bargained away by you or your spouse. This means simply that any agreement made between the spouses for support of the children may be completely disregarded by the court.

This right to support can quite easily be enforced by the family court. All support orders made by the Ontario Court (General Division) or the Ontario Court (Provincial Division) are enforced by automatic payroll deduction through the government payroll office of the Family Support Plan. Certain forms must be filed with your other documents to make sure this is done. Payments usually continue until the children are 18 years of age, become self-supporting, or marry, whichever event occurs first. Children who are not married or self-supporting and who remain in school past the age of 18, up to and including three years of post-secondary school, would also be entitled to support.

You will note from reading section 2, subsection (d) of the Divorce Act, that in divorce proceedings children have a basic right to support up to the age of 16 years. However, support may continue beyond this age if the children are unable to provide for themselves and are dependent on either the husband or the wife. Obviously, the age to which children remain entitled to support varies from case to case. Generally speaking, a child is not entitled to support beyond the age of 18 years.

An order of support for either you or the children of the marriage can be varied at any time if there has been a material change in circumstances. The onus of proving a material change in circumstances lies on the applicant.

The jurisdiction to hear and determine a variation proceeding rests in the court of a province where either former spouse is ordinarily a resident at the commencement of the variation proceeding or in a court whose jurisdiction is accepted by both spouses. An application to vary or suspend a support order or any term of an order may be brought by either or both former spouses. The Divorce Act gives the courts the power to vary or suspend a spousal or child support order retroactively. This allows a court to eliminate support arrears that may have fallen due.

A support order may be for a fixed term or until the occurrence of a specific event, such as the remarriage of the spouse receiving support. The act imposes strict limitations on the court's ability to make a variation order after the expiration of the fixed term or the occurrence of the stipulated event.

The court must be satisfied that a variation order is necessary to relieve economic hardship arising from a change that is related to the marriage and that the changed circumstances would have resulted in a different order had they occurred at the time the original order was made. Hardship that arises from circumstances unconnected with the marriage, such as the inability to find a job, would not support a variation order. If, for example, after the fixed term you lose your job because of economic conditions, this will not allow you to return to the courts for a variation of a fixed-term support order.

Keep in mind that the courts are reluctant to interfere with the terms of a negotiated settlement. This is particularly true where the settlement is supposed to finally resolve all property and support rights between the parties. A court will intervene, however, where a change of circumstances makes the settlement unjust.

There is no requirement in the act for the court to vary a support order if one of the spouses remarries or begins living with someone. The remarriage or cohabitation of a divorced spouse is a relevant but not a decisive factor on any subsequent application to vary a support order.

It is very important to note that in an application for support, the conduct of the parties is irrelevant. However, the persistent failure of a financially dependent spouse to acquire the skills necessary to achieve economic self-sufficiency may constitute a basis for the variation or suspension of a support order, as one of the objectives of the Divorce Act is to put each party in a position where they are economically self-sufficient.

2. The Family Law Act

If you do not wish to immediately petition for divorce, or if you wish to obtain a division of property, you may decide to commence proceedings under the Family Law Act, which is provincial legislation. This act requires that when support or division of property is involved, the petitioner and the respondent must file a financial information form.

Some people find the relationship between the Family Law Act and the Divorce Act very confusing. Consider, for instance, the situation where you and your spouse separate and you wish to have exclusive possession of the matrimonial home, custody of the children, and support for you and the children. You have not yet made the decision to apply for a divorce. In this instance you should retain the services of a lawyer and he or she will commence an action on your behalf under the Family Law Act for relief such as exclusive possession of the matrimonial home, custody, equalization of net family property, and support for you and the children. It is hoped you will eventually resolve these particular issues by agreement or court order and then, if you so desire, divorce proceedings can be initiated.

In this case, the only issue in the divorce proceedings will be the grounds for the actual divorce; all other matters will have been determined under the Family Law Act. The minutes of settlement, separation agreement, or court order that has disposed of the Family Law Act proceedings will be part of the record before the court in the divorce action, and the final Divorce Judgment will incorporate any appropriate provisions of this agreement.

The Family Law Act also applies to cases where a claim to property is being made. Because the Divorce Act is federal legislation and the federal government has no jurisdiction over property rights, the property claim must be made through provincial legislation or the Family Law Act. The claim, however, must be made in the Ontario Court (General Division). If you and your spouse separate and you decide to apply for a divorce immediately, your Petition for Divorce must state that you are also commencing Family Law Act proceedings to claim an equalization of net family property. Again, if you decide to go this route, the services of a lawyer are recommended.

3. Canada Pension Plan benefits

A divorced person may be entitled to share Canada Pension Plan credits with his or her former spouse. A division of pension credits may increase a person's benefit or even create one where none previously existed.

Eligibility for credit splitting depends on the length of your relationship, when it ended, if there was a marriage agreement, and other factors. For more information on CPP credit splitting, contact the Income Security Programs office nearest you.

4. Separation agreements

As many individuals do not want to start divorce proceedings immediately, they often seek advice about being "legally separated." Practically speaking, a husband and wife are legally separated when they are simply living apart.

In a situation where the husband and wife are living apart, they would often be well advised to have a lawyer write what is commonly called a "separation agreement." Such an agreement is simply a contract between a husband and wife determining certain issues such as support, custody of children, and the division of assets. This document sets out the rights and obligations of the parties but does not make the separation any more "legal."

Before such an agreement can be entered into, certain issues have to be settled between the parties. You should consider the following matters:

(a) A clause should be inserted that stipulates that neither party will annoy, molest, or interfere with the other.

(b) If there are children of the marriage, agreement should be reached about custody and access.

(c) The issue of support for the children should be agreed on, including the amount to be paid and the age to which payments will continue. When discussing this matter with your spouse, you should also consider the requirements of the children beyond high school and, in particular, the question of financial assistance to the children should they wish to attend post-secondary institutions. While an agreement covering support payments for the children may have little effect in family court, the matter should nevertheless be discussed by the parties and agreed on if possible.

(d) If there are assets such as cars, investments, and furnishings, an agreement will have to be reached for disposing of them.

(e) If there is a family home, agreement should be reached about whether —

(i) the house will be sold and the proceeds of the sale divided equally between the parties;

(ii) one party will buy out the other; or

(iii) one party will continue to live in the home with the children until the family is grown and self-supporting. If the wife is to have sole custody of the children, it is often agreed that she will continue to live in the family home with them. In this case, definite agreement should be reached about who will pay for the mortgage and for major repairs, such as a new roof or new furnace, which might be required from time to time.

(f) If one spouse is claiming support and the other agrees to pay, then some provision should be included in the agreement on the amount to be paid, the times of payments, and under what circumstances the payments will cease (e.g., remarriage or the supported spouse living with another person).

(g) If there are debts outstanding prior to the separation of the parties, there should be a clause in the agreement stating who is responsible for such debts. Provision should also be made for indemnifying each party against responsibility for debts incurred by the other after the agreement has been signed.

(h) There should be a clause in the agreement determining the effective period of the agreement (e.g., whether it is to be an interim agreement to be terminated on dissolution of the marriage, or whether it is to continue in effect after a divorce judgment has been granted), particularly in regard to property settlement and support for the spouse and children.

The best way to approach the drafting of a separation agreement is for you and your spouse to sit down and discuss the issues mentioned above. There will undoubtedly be other matters to consider, but the issues set out should be your first considerations.

If you can reach agreement on these basic issues, I suggest that you then retain a lawyer to put in writing what you and your spouse have already agreed on. Then your spouse must retain a lawyer for the sole purpose of providing him or her with independent legal advice on how the agreement affects his or her rights.

You must remember, however, that the separation agreement is, in fact, a contract, and it is presumed that the parties know and thoroughly understand what they are entering into. While you and your spouse should talk over the main areas of the proposed agreement beforehand, if support for you and/or your children is involved, you should see a lawyer.

It is essential to keep in mind that a separation agreement may not be enforceable and therefore may not be worth the paper it is printed on if, for example, one party was forced to sign it, if there was incomplete disclosure of assets, if the effect of the agreement is grossly unfair, or if both spouses have not had independent legal advice. The chances of having a worthless separation agreement may be too great for you to take the chance of doing it yourself.

Remember, whatever you are told about your rights, it is up to you to decide whether or not you want to exercise them to their fullest extent.

c. TAX ASPECTS OF SEPARATION AND DIVORCE

1. Support payments

If you are planning to separate or have already done so and support payments are involved for your spouse or children, you should take time to read this section. Until very recently, the philosophy of the tax department was to allow one person to deduct if the other included the income for tax purposes in his or her return. You should, however, be aware of the following required formalities (and see the **important note** at the end of this section).

If you agree to pay monthly support (called "periodic payments") to your spouse and/or children, you will be able to deduct those payments when calculating your taxable income if —

(a) the payments are made according to a court order, Divorce Judgment, or a written agreement;

(b) the payments are made by you to your spouse or his or her children, or in certain circumstances, to a third party (such as a mortgage company) for the benefit of the spouse or children, on a periodic basis (note that these third-party expenses must be specifically identified in the document creating the obligation to pay);

(c) you are separated from your spouse at the time the first payment is made and remain separated throughout the year; and

(d) you were legally married, or you and your spouse are of opposite sexes and have cohabited continuously in a common-law situation for three years or more, or are cohabiting and have a child. In common-law situations, the payments must be made pursuant to an order of the court.

As has been said, the support payments are deductible only if they are periodic in nature, for example, $500 per month for a spouse during his or her lifetime. A lump sum support payment such as a once and for all payment of $10 000 in lieu of future support claims is not deductible. Neither is it included in the recipient's income for tax purposes.

As you can see, it is important to define in your separation agreement that you will pay a specific amount of support at regular intervals, for example, biweekly or monthly. This will ensure that payments are properly deductible.

Your agreement can be worded in such a way as to allow tax deductions for payments made prior to the date of the agreement. This has certain limitations. Payments made in the year in which the agreement is signed and for the previous 12 months are deductible, but you cannot go back further than that. In other words, if an agreement is signed in May 1995 and specifies that prior payments are deductible, then those prior payments going back only as far as January 1, 1994, can be deducted. When filing your tax returns, always be certain to include a copy of your agreement or court order.

Also, if you are considering reconciling with your spouse, you may lose the deduction for the year unless you remain separated "throughout the remainder of the year." To give a simple illustration, if you and your spouse separated according to a written agreement in February, and the two of you got back together for the month of November in an attempt to reconcile, you would not be able to claim support payments as a deduction because you were not separated "throughout the remainder of the year." A reconciliation attempted in January of the following year would be more beneficial — at least financially.

Remember, if you are able to deduct support payments, your spouse will have to include the same amount in his or her income. In the above example, however, as you were not able to deduct the payments made from February through to November, your spouse would not have to claim them as income.

Important note: The federal government has passed a series of changes to the tax treatment of child support payments for those whose separation agreement or court order is made after May 1997. Recipients will no longer include such payments in their income; payors will not claim a deduction for the payments. Child support payments will be determined net of tax, in accordance with a schedule of child support guidelines which are shown in Table #1.

2. Single parents

Your family situation can have a great impact on the amount of income tax that you have to pay each year. If you are separated or divorced you may have some special tax complications that do not affect the majority of the population, especially if there are children involved. The income tax department's free booklet *Income Tax and the Single Parent* provides useful information for these situations.

The amount of personal exemptions that single parents can claim is a complicated issue, especially in the year that a divorce or separation occurs. Support payments, family allowance payments, claims for child care expenses, and the income tax aspects of various kinds of property settlements should all be checked carefully.

If you are divorced or separated during the year and both you and your spouse have taxable income to report and children who were dependent on one of you for part of the year and on the other for part of the year, it is possible that a double claim may be made for each child.

3. The child tax credit

Everybody who claims the child tax credit must also file a personal income tax return.

A Schedule 10 must be completely filled out and sent in with the personal income tax return, even though the person claiming the credit may have no income to report. If the form is not submitted there will be no government refund cheque.

The basis on which the child tax credit is determined is the family's "net income." Net income for purposes of the credit is exactly the same as the figure on your personal income tax return. The child tax credit form requires the net income of both spouses and the signature of both spouses indicating that the information is "true and correct."

This requirement may cause some problems if you are separated and your spouse refuses to co-operate. If it proves impossible to get the necessary information about your spouse's income, you should attach a note to your claim explaining the problem, and the tax department will pull your spouse's file and make the correct adjustments.

This advice applies, too, if you are divorced and unable to obtain a signature from your former spouse.

When claiming the credit for the year in which your divorce takes place, you should include the net income of your spouse only up to the day on which the divorce was made final.

4. Child care expenses

If you are a single parent, divorced, or separated, and if you have children to care for, you will probably want to claim child care expenses. Remember, though, that you can make a claim only if you report income from employment, self-employment, adult training allowances, or some form of grant; these expenses must have been incurred and paid in the taxation year in Canada. You do not have to file receipts, but you should keep them in case the tax department wants to see them.

TABLE #1
MONTHLY CHILD SUPPORT PAYMENTS FROM MAY 1997

1996 Annual Gross Income	Monthy amounts based on number of children (in dollars)					
	One	Two	Three	Four	Five	Six or More
0 - 6 754	0	0	0	0	0	0
6 755 - 7 000	8	9	10	11	11	11
7 001 - 8 000	40	45	50	55	55	55
8 001 - 9 000	71	80	89	99	99	99
9 001 - 10 000	79	93	106	120	120	120
10 001 - 12 000	109	148	170	192	192	192
12 001 - 14 000	119	202	232	262	262	262
14 001 - 16 000	131	238	293	332	332	332
16 001 - 18 000	143	261	355	402	402	402
18 001 - 20 000	166	285	388	472	472	472
20 001 - 22 000	197	308	420	512	542	542
22 001 - 24 000	217	338	452	551	612	612
24 001 - 26 000	235	378	484	590	678	682
26 001 - 28 000	249	413	515	623	718	743
28 001 - 30 000	262	439	554	655	755	800
30 001 - 32 000	273	457	585	686	782	839
32 001 - 34 000	288	481	625	734	818	887
34 001 - 36 000	304	506	666	784	867	937
36 001 - 38 000	319	531	699	835	919	988
38 001 - 40 000	335	555	730	873	970	1 040
40 001 - 42 000	350	579	762	911	1 022	1 092
42 001 - 44 000	366	603	793	948	1 074	1 143
44 001 - 46 000	382	628	825	987	1 120	1 233
46 001 - 48 000	398	653	858	1 025	1 164	1 280
48 001 - 50 000	414	679	890	1 063	1 207	1 328
50 001 - 52 000	430	704	922	1 101	1 250	1 376
52 001 - 54 000	444	726	952	1 137	1 290	1 420
54 001 - 56 000	458	748	981	1 171	1 330	1 464
56 001 - 58 000	473	772	1 012	1 208	1 371	1 509
58 001 - 60 000	488	795	1 041	1 242	1 410	1 552
60 001 - 62 000	501	817	1 069	1 275	1 447	1 592
62 001 - 64 000	515	838	1 096	1 308	1 483	1 633
64 001 - 66 000	528	858	1 122	1 338	1 519	1 671
66 001 - 68 000	540	878	1 149	1 370	1 554	1 710

TABLE #1 — Continued

1996 Annual Gross Income	Monthy amounts based on number of children (in dollars)					
	One	Two	Three	Four	Five	Six or More
68 001 - 70 000	553	898	1 174	1 400	1 588	1 748
70 001 - 72 000	565	918	1 199	1 430	1 623	1 785
72 001 - 74 000	578	938	1 225	1 461	1 657	1 823
74 001 - 76 000	591	958	1 251	1 492	1 692	1 861
76 001 - 78 000	604	978	1 278	1 523	1 727	1 899
78 001 - 80 000	617	998	1 303	1 553	1 761	1 937
80 001 - 82 000	630	1 018	1 330	1 584	1 796	1 975
82 001 - 84 000	643	1 039	1 355	1 615	1 830	2 013
84 001 - 86 000	656	1 059	1 381	1 645	1 865	2 051
86 001 - 88 000	669	1 079	1 408	1 676	1 900	2 089
88 001 - 90 000	682	1 099	1 433	1 707	1 935	2 127
90 001 - 92 000	695	1 120	1 460	1 738	1 969	2 165
92 001 - 94 000	708	1 140	1 485	1 768	2 004	2 203
94 001 - 96 000	721	1 160	1 512	1 799	2 039	2 241
96 001 - 98 000	734	1 180	1 538	1 830	2 073	2 279
98 001 - 100 000	747	1 200	1 563	1 860	2 108	2 318
100 001 - 102 000	760	1 221	1 590	1 891	2 143	2 355
102 001 - 104 000	773	1 241	1 615	1 922	2 177	2 393
104 001 - 106 000	786	1 261	1 642	1 953	2 212	2 431
106 001 - 108 000	799	1 281	1 668	1 983	2 247	2 470
108 001 - 110 000	812	1 302	1 693	2 014	2 281	2 508
110 001 - 112 000	825	1 322	1 720	2 045	2 316	2 545
112 001 - 114 000	838	1 342	1 745	2 075	2 351	2 583
114 001 - 116 000	851	1 363	1 772	2 106	2 385	2 621
116 001 - 118 000	864	1 383	1 798	2 137	2 420	2 660
118 001 - 120 000	877	1 403	1 824	2 168	2 455	2 698
120 001 - 122 000	890	1 423	1 850	2 199	2 490	2 735
122 001 - 124 000	903	1 443	1 875	2 229	2 524	2 773
124 001 - 126 000	916	1 463	1 902	2 260	2 559	2 812
126 001 - 128 000	929	1 484	1 928	2 291	2 593	2 850
128 001 - 130 000	942	1 504	1 954	2 322	2 628	2 888
130 001 - 132 000	955	1 524	1 980	2 352	2 663	2 925
132 001 - 134 000	968	1 545	2 005	2 383	2 698	2 963
134 001 - 136 000	981	1 565	2 032	2 414	2 732	3 002

TABLE #1 — Continued

1996 Annual Gross Income	Monthy amounts based on number of children (in dollars)					
	One	Two	Three	Four	Five	Six or More
136 001 - 138 000	994	1 585	2 058	2 445	2 767	3 040
138 001 - 140 000	1 007	1 605	2 084	2 475	2 802	3 078
140 001 - 142 000	1 020	1 625	2 110	2 506	2 836	3 115
142 001 - 144 000	1 033	1 645	2 136	2 537	2 871	3 154
144 001 - 146 000	1 046	1 666	2 162	2 568	2 905	3 192
146 001 - 148 000	1 059	1 686	2 188	2 598	2 940	3 230
148 001 - 150 000	1 072	1 706	2 214	2 629	2 975	3 268
150 001 +	1 072 plus 0.71% of excess	1 706 plus 1.14% of excess	2 214 plus 1.48% of excess	2 629 plus 1.75% of excess	2 975 plus 1.98% of excess	3 268 plus 2.18% of excess

Children for whom you claim must not be over 16 years of age in the taxation year, unless they are infirm, and you may not deduct child care payments to anyone you or your spouse claim as a dependant or to a relative who is under 21. If you are claiming payments being made to a boarding school or camp, the maximum allowance is $30 per week per child.

Only those expenses incurred to allow the parent to work, to take occupational training courses, or to do research work (if grants are received) are claimable. Babysitting expenses incurred for other purposes, such as attending school, usually don't qualify.

The tax department publishes a pamphlet called *Child Care Expenses* which is available free from any district taxation office.

4
PRELIMINARY NOTES ON PROCEDURE

a. GENERAL

All documents submitted to court must be on letter-size paper. It is permissible to use any type of bond paper except the easily erasable type, which is not acceptable at the court office. (Any stationer will help you select the proper type of paper.)

Photocopies are acceptable and you should, wherever possible, type one original only and then photocopy this original to obtain the desired number of copies. If you do not have access to a photocopying machine, carbon copies are, of course, still acceptable. However, even though the documents may be photocopied, you must personally sign all copies. You must not photocopy your signature; it will not be accepted.

Note: Certain types of photocopies are not acceptable to the court. (Xerox and other dry copiers are acceptable.) If you plan to use "wet" photocopies, take a sample copy to your local court or registrar's office and ask if it is acceptable. Only the kind that have passed the 20-year preservation test will be approved by the courts; be certain that the kind you plan to use fits into this category. Most copies now pass the test.

b. TITLE OF PROCEEDING

All legal documents must have a heading known as the "title of proceeding." This allows documents to be properly identified. Specifically, the title of proceeding in a divorce action will contain the following information:

(a) The court registry number, which will be stamped or written on the original and all copies of the Petition when it is filed, and which should be used on all subsequent documents filed in the registrar's office

(b) Name of the court, Ontario Court (General Division)

(c) Full names of the petitioner and the respondent (or husband and wife if you are joint petitioners)

The title of proceeding should head all of your documents. In many of the examples I refer simply to "title of proceeding." When preparing all your documents, head them with a title of proceeding similar to that shown in Sample #1.

c. BACKING SHEETS
(Document backs)

Every document filed in the registrar's office is required to have a document back, which is an extra page placed behind the last page of your document. It has the title of proceedings, the name of the particular document, and the name, address, and telephone number of the petitioner — or, in the case of a Joint Petition, of the husband and wife — typed on it.

A document back is shown in Sample #2. Note that the title of proceedings is typed across the top of the page, and the title of the document, etc. is typed down the right-hand side.

If you are typing your own documents and document backs, position the information in the same way that is shown in

Sample #2. The backing pages face outward and are attached to the complete document.

All documents submitted to the registrar's office for filing must have backs. The only exception to this rule will be when you file what is called your Record. It is not necessary to include copies of the backs of the documents in the Record.

d. IDENTIFICATION OF JUDGES

This section applies only if a court appearance is necessary. The Ontario Court (General Division) has exclusive jurisdiction to hear divorce cases and the registrar of the court will help you process the paperwork for doing this.

When the matter is being heard before a judge, he or she will be referred to in the Judgment for Divorce as "The Honourable Mr. or Mdm. Justice_____."

e. FORMAT FOR COURT ORDER

In addition to the requirement to use ordinary bond paper (not the easily erasable type) for your orders, it is essential that when you prepare and submit any order for the approval of the court, you leave three to four inches (about seven to ten centimetres) of space at the bottom of the document. This space is required for the stamps and signatures of various officials as well as the judge. There have been occasions where orders submitted by lawyers have been rejected because insufficient space was allowed for the stamps and signatures.

It is also necessary to allow a one-and-a-half- to two-inch margin (four to five centimetres) on the left side of your documents. This is also to allow for any necessary registry stamps and/or notations.

Note: All typewritten documents submitted to the court must be double-spaced.

SAMPLE #1
TITLE OF PROCEEDING

Court file no._____

ONTARIO COURT (GENERAL DIVISION)

BETWEEN:

Joan Public   PETITIONER
                                               (Wife   )

- and -

(Court seal)

John Que Public

                                               RESPONDENT
                                               (Husband   )

Joan Que Public   and   John Que Public

PETITIONER(Wife   )   RESPONDENT(Husband   )

(Short title of proceeding)

Court file no. _____

ONTARIO COURT
(GENERAL DIVISION)

Proceedings commenced at

(NAME OF DOCUMENT)

Name, address, and telephone number of petitioner.

Joan Public
322 Lakeshore Road
Toronto, Ontario
555-5666

Petitioner appearing in person

5

STEP-BY-STEP PROCEDURE

If you have decided that your situation is simple enough for you to do your divorce yourself, and you can foresee no complications with proof, etc., you are now ready to begin the step-by-step procedure. (See Appendix 1 for a detailed checklist of steps.)

Samples of the forms you will have to submit are illustrated in this chapter. (**Note:** If you and/or your spouse live in Hamilton, London, Barrie, Kingston, and/or Napanee, you are in an area under the jurisdiction of the Ontario Court (General Division) Family Court, formerly the Unified Family Court and you may have to file different forms. See chapter 6). If you are confused by any section of a form, seek professional advice. Do not proceed if you are uncertain; the consequences of making an error could be costly.

a. OBTAINING YOUR MARRIAGE REGISTRATION

The Certificate of Marriage given to you at the time of your marriage may not be adequate for proving the marriage in court.

If you were married in Canada or in a country that is a member of the Commonwealth, you should get a copy of the registration of your marriage. If you were married in Ontario, write to the Office of the Registrar General, P.O. Box 4600, Thunder Bay, Ontario, P7B 6L8. If you were married outside the province, refer to Appendix 2 for a list of addresses to write to for your copy. This copy no longer needs to be certified.

The cost of this copy of registration in Ontario is currently $15*. Send a certified cheque, or money order, payable to the Minister of Finance with a letter including the following particulars:

(a) Full name of wife (maiden name)

(b) Full name of husband

(c) Date of marriage

(d) Place of marriage

b. FOREIGN MARRIAGES

If you were married in a country other than Canada, the United States, or a Commonwealth country, you will be required to prove the validity of your marriage certificate. This is usually done by having the document translated under oath by a translator and by having that translator's certificate attached.

A lawyer or legal aid office will be able to supply the name of a translator who is accustomed to providing this service. In most cases, a motion concerning the admissibility of the affidavit must also be made.

If you are at all uncertain of what to do in this slightly complicated situation, I suggest that you consult a lawyer for this purpose only. Don't forget to get a quotation for the fee. It should cost about $100.

c. PREPARATION OF JOINT PETITION

The Petition shown in Sample #3 is a Joint Petition and is to be used when *both* spouses jointly seek a Divorce Judgment. It is important to note that a Joint Petition can be used *only* under section 8(2)(a) of the Divorce Act (i.e., one-year separation). If

---

Note that all fees are subject to change without notice. Please check all fees with the court or appropriate government office before submitting funds.

you want to proceed under section 8(2)(b) (i.e., adultery or cruelty), you must file as a sole petitioner. Also, a Joint Petition can be used only when a divorce is sought on consent of both parties. That means if you and your spouse disagree on any issue, such as custody, access, or support, you must not use a Joint Petition.

In a Joint Petition, the parties are simply referred to as "husband" and "wife." All claims must be agreed to by both spouses. The divorce will be granted to both spouses.

You will require the original and two copies of the Joint Petition for divorce. Therefore, if you purchase the set of forms available from the publisher (see page x), you should use one set from the package for rough work, one set for the final copy, and then photocopy two further copies (one for each of you) *before signing.* Then you must sign each copy as though it were an original. It is not absolutely necessary that both parties sign the Joint Petition; however, it is recommended.

Refer to Sample #3 while drafting your own Joint Petition. Make certain that your name and your spouse's name are *exactly* as set out in the marriage certificate or marriage registration. If a woman elected to retain her maiden name, this will be noted on the marriage documents and should be used on the Petition. If you or your spouse are known by any other name, set out the names as follows:

John Que Public,
also known as
John Que Private

1. Explanatory notes for completing a Joint Petition

Complete all relevant sections of the Petition as briefly and concisely as possible. Refer to examples that set out the basic pleadings for particulars of your grounds for divorce. The following sections correspond to the sections in the Petition for Divorce.

Paragraph 1 — Joint Petition

Set out exactly the relief you are seeking. If you are asking the court to ratify other orders such as custody or support or the division of property that you and your spouse have agreed to on consent, you may set out these other terms in subparagraph 1(b).

Under subparagraph 1(c), or under the Family Law Act, you may also ask the court to recognize consent arrangements to custody, access, and support. It is wise to list these things under 1(b) and under 1(c). Should the court then not grant your divorce for some reason, you will still be entitled to an order granting the other relief.

You must consider exactly what relief you want the court to grant, and ask for it. As you can see on the sample, your Petition first claims that you and your spouse should be divorced from each other. Other common orders sought in a Joint Petition are the following:

(a) Custody of the infant child(ren) of the marriage with reasonable access to the spouse. If custody is claimed, you may claim "reasonable access," or if access is to be specified, you must set out in paragraph 24 the actual access agreed upon. For example:

> The husband and wife have agreed that the husband shall have access to the children on alternate weekends, one week during the Christmas holidays, and one month during the summer vacation.

> **Note:** The terms of access will be included in the Divorce Judgment.

(b) Reasonable access to the infant child(ren).

(c) Support for the husband/wife and the said infant child(ren) in the amount of $_____.

Be absolutely certain whether or not you wish to claim support or division of property for yourself before issuing the Petition. If no order for support for you (exclusive

Court file no._____

ONTARIO COURT (GENERAL DIVISION)

John Que Public   HUSBAND

(Court seal)

and

Joan Que Public   WIFE

JOINT PETITION FOR DIVORCE

Date_____Issued by_____
                                                                     Local registrar

Address of court office
393 University Avenue
Toronto, Ontario
M5G 1E6

JOINT PETITION

State precisely everything you want the court to include in the judgment. Everything you want to include must have been agreed to by both spouses. If you want to include provisions of a separation agreement in the judgment, refer to the specific provisions to be included.

1.   The husband and wife jointly seek:

    (a)   a divorce;

    ~~(b)   under the Divorce Act,~~

        (i)

INTERNATIONAL SELF-COUNSEL PRESS LTD.
1481 Charlotte Road
North Vancouver, B.C. V7J 1H1
DIVONT-JOINT(1-1) 91

If relief is claimed on consent under any other Act, refer to the Act in the claim.

(c)   under the Family Law Act,

(i)

GROUNDS FOR DIVORCE — SEPARATION

2.   · The spouses have lived separate and apart since ___June 1, 199-_____ .

Date

The spouses have resumed cohabitation during the following periods in an unsuccessful attempt at reconciliation:

Date(s) of cohabitation

If none, state "none."

None

INTERNATIONAL SELF-COUNSEL PRESS LTD.
1481 Charlotte Road
North Vancouver, B.C. V7J 1H1
DIVONT-JOINT(1-2) 91

RECONCILIATION

3. There is no possibility of reconciliation of the spouses.

4. The following efforts to reconcile have been made:

State details. Where no efforts have been made, state "none."

None

DETAILS OF MARRIAGE

Where possible, copy the information from the marriage certificate.

5. Date of marriage: December 27, 1984

6. Place of marriage: Toronto, Ontario
   (City, town, or municipality, province or state, country)

7. Wife's surname immediately before marriage: Jones

8. Wife's surname at birth: Jones

9. Husband's surname immediately before marriage: Public

10. Husband's surname at birth: Public

11. Marital status of husband at time of marriage: Never married
    (Never married, divorced, or widower)

12. Marital status of wife at time of marriage: Never married
    (Never married, divorced, or widow)

13. Wife's birthplace: Toronto, Ontario
    (City, town, or municipality, province or state, country)

14. Wife's birthdate: April 11, 1955

15. Husband's birthplace: Calgary, Alberta
    (City, town, or municipality, province or state, country)

16. Husband's birthdate: May 12, 1954

Check one of (a), (b), or (c) and complete as required.

17. (a) [X] A certificate of ☐ the marriage [X] the registration of the marriage of the spouses has been filed with the court

    (b) ☐ It is impossible to obtain a certificate of the marriage or its registration because:

    (c) ☐ A certificate of the marriage or its registration will be filed before this action is set down for trial or a motion is made for judgment.

INTERNATIONAL SELF-COUNSEL PRESS LTD.
1481 Charlotte Road
North Vancouver, B.C. V7J 1H1
DIVONT JOINT (1-3) 91

RESIDENCE

18. The wife has resided in: _Toronto, Ontario_

    (City, town, or municipality, province or state, country)

    _____ since _birth_

    (Date)

19. The husband has resided in: _Toronto, Ontario_

    (City, town, or municipality, province or state, country)

    _____ since _December, 1982_

    (Date)

20. The husband's current address is: _1000 Yonge Street, Toronto, Ontario_

    The wife's current address is: _322 Lakeshore Road, Toronto, Ontario_

Check appropriate box or boxes.

21. The ⊠ husband ⊠ wife has habitually resided in Ontario for at least one year immediately preceding the commencement of this proceeding.

CHILDREN

22. The following are all the living children of the marriage as defined by the Divorce Act:

Full name	Birthdate	School and grade or year	Person with whom child lives and length of time child has lived there

There are no children of the marriage.

The children ordinarily reside in: _____

(City, town, or municipality, province or state, country)

Be sure that this paragraph agrees with the claim under 1. above.

23. (a) The spouses seek an order on consent for custody or joint custody of the following children on the following terms:

    Name of child   Terms of the order

    Not applicable

INTERNATIONAL SELF-COUNSEL PRESS LTD.
1481 Charlotte Road
North Vancouver, B.C. V7J 1H1
DIVONT JOINT(1-4) 91

SAMPLE #3 — Continued

(b) The spouses are not seeking an order for custody and

☐ are content that a previous order for custody remain in force

☐ are attempting to obtain an order for custody in another proceeding full particulars of which are as follows:

7(c) . The spouses seek an order on consent for access (visiting arrangements) to the following children on the following terms:

Name of child   Terms of the order

INTERNATIONAL SELF-COUNSEL PRESS LTD.
1481 Charlotte Road
North Vancouver, B.C. V7J 1H1
DIVONT-JOINT(1-5) 91

State details such as days of the week, hours of visit, and place of access.

24. ~~(a) The following are the existing visiting arrangements (access) for the spouse who does not have the children living~~ with him or her.

INTERNATIONAL SELF-COUNSEL PRESS LTD.
1481 Charlotte Road
North Vancouver, B.C. V7J 1H1
DIVONT-JOINT(1-8) 91

SAMPLE #3 — Continued

Check appropriate box.

(b) The existing visiting arrangements (access) are: ☐ satisfactory ☐ not satisfactory

If not satisfactory, give reasons and describe how the arrangements should be changed.

25. The order sought in paragraph 23 is in the best interests of the children for the following reasons:

26. The following material changes in the circumstances of the spouses are expected to affect the children, their custody, and the visiting arrangements (access) in the future:

INTERNATIONAL SELF-COUNSEL PRESS LTD.
1481 Charlotte Road
North Vancouver, B.C. V7J 1H1
DIVONT-JOINT(1-7) 91

27. (a) The existing arrangements between the spouses for support for the children are as follows:

Amount paid	Time period (Weekly, monthly, etc.)	Paid by (Husband or wife)	Paid for (Name of child)

Check appropriate box.

If not being honoured, specify how much is unpaid and for how long. If you agree on an order for payment of part or all of the unpaid amount, be sure to include it

(b) The existing support arrangements ☐ are being honoured ☐ are not being honoured.

Be sure that this paragraph agrees with the claim under 1. above.

(c) The spouses propose that the support arrangements for the children should be as follows:

Amount to be paid	Time period (Weekly, monthly, etc.)	To be paid by (Husband or wife)	To be paid for (Name of child)

Check appropriate box.

If not being met, state particulars.

28. The education needs of the children ☐ are being met ☐ are not being met.

INTERNATIONAL SELF-COUNSEL PRESS LTD.
1481 Charlotte Road
North Vancouver, B.C. V7J 1H1
DIVONT-JOINT(1-8) 91

OTHER COURT PROCEEDINGS

State the name of the court, the court file number, the kind of order the court was asked to make, and what order, if any, the court made. If the proceeding is not yet completed, state its current status.

29. The following are all other court proceedings with reference to the marriage or any child of the marriage:

None

DOMESTIC CONTRACTS AND FINANCIAL ARRANGEMENTS

Indicate whether the contract or arrangement is now in effect, and if support payments are not being paid in full, state the amount that has not been paid.

30. The spouses have entered into the following domestic contracts and other written or oral financial arrangements:

Date	Nature of contract or arrangement	Status

None

NO COLLUSION

31. There has been no collusion in relation to this divorce proceeding.

INTERNATIONAL SELF-COUNSEL PRESS LTD.
1481 Charlotte Road
North Vancouver, B.C. V7J 1H1
DIVONT-JOINT(1-9) 91

DECLARATION OF SPOUSES

32.

(a) I have read and understand this petition for divorce. The statements in it are true, to the best of my knowledge, information, and belief.

(b) I understand that I have the right to seek independent legal advice concerning this proceeding and to retain my own separate counsel.

(c) I understand that I may lose my right to make a claim for division of property after the divorce if I do not make the claim at this time.

Date _May 2, 199-_____ _John Q. Public_____
(Signature of husband)

Date _May 2, 199-_____ _Joan Public_____
(Signature of wife)

INTERNATIONAL SELF-COUNSEL PRESS LTD.
1481 Charlotte Road
North Vancouver, B.C. V7J 1H1
DIVONT-JOINT(1-10) 91

of payments for the children) or division of property is set out in the Judgment, you will not later be able to apply for such relief in the divorce action. However, you may still have property or support rights under the Family Law Act. If you intend to pursue these rights in separate proceedings after your divorce has been finalized, you would be well advised to consult a lawyer prior to getting a divorce judgment.

Paragraph 2 — Grounds for divorce — Separation

In paragraph 2, fill in the appropriate date indicating when your separation began. Also indicate with dates the beginning and end of any periods during which you and your spouse resumed cohabitation.

Paragraphs 3 and 4 — Reconciliation

If no efforts have been made to reconcile, simply indicate this with the words "there have been no attempts at reconciliation" or "none."

If reconciliation has been attempted, indicate this concisely. Here is an example:

> The parties hereto went to a marriage counsellor in July 19—, but were not able to effect a reconciliation.

Paragraphs 5 to 17 — Details of marriage

Remember, Petitions will not normally be accepted for filing unless your marriage certificate or a copy of the registration of your marriage is filed as well. The registrar has the discretion to accept the Petition, however, if there is a valid reason for your inability to file a certificate or copy of registration and that reason is stated in paragraph 17(b).

Paragraphs 18 to 21 — Residence

If either you or your spouse has been ordinarily resident in Ontario for at least one year before the Petition is issued, the court has the jurisdiction to grant a divorce.

Paragraphs 22 to 28 — Children

All children who are under 16 years of age or those over 16 but dependent on either spouse due to illness, disability, because they are still attending school (generally up to the age of 22), or other cause should be listed in the Petition with their places and dates of birth.

If there are children of your marriage, the court must be satisfied that proper support arrangements have been made before a divorce is granted. Remember, if you and your spouse disagree about child custody or financial arrangements, you *cannot* use the Joint Petition procedure.

In paragraph 23, fill in the particulars of the request of your custody order to agree with your claim under paragraph 1 of the Petition. If you had a child, the terms of the order might read:

> Custody to the wife. Reasonable access to the husband.

If there is a child or children, paragraph 25 would be completed with wording such as:

> (i) Since the child's birth, the husband and wife have shared responsibility for his care.
>
> (ii) The father's occupation as a long-distance bus driver requires him to travel frequently.
>
> (iii) The wife is in a better position to meet the day-to-day needs of the child.
>
> (iv) The child has a close relationship with both parents.

Paragraph 27 must be completed if there is a claim for support. The court must be satisfied that reasonable arrangements have been made for the support of any children before a divorce will be granted, and you must set out financial particulars in sufficient detail to allow the court to reach this conclusion.

Paragraph 29 — Other court proceedings

This section includes matters such as family court support hearings or actions for judicial separation, custody, or annulment.

If you were involved in any such proceedings, indicate when the matter was heard, and the results. If there is a previous action still not completed, consult a lawyer so that it can be disposed of.

Paragraph 30 — Domestic contracts and financial arrangements

Set out the date of any pertinent agreements, either written or verbal, such as a marriage contract as defined by the Family Law Act, a separation agreement, or a financial arrangement.

Paragraph 31 — No collusion

If you are guilty of collusion (see Glossary for a definition of this term), your divorce will be refused. If you feel you may have a problem complying with this requirement, you should consult a lawyer.

Paragraph 32 — Declaration of spouses

This paragraph calls for a declaration of spouses; simply sign where indicated. Since both parties sign the Petition, obviously the document need not be served. To complete your Petition, date the document and complete the document back.

2. Preparing the other documents

Once you have completed the Petition, you must prepare these other documents:

(a) Notice of Motion (see Sample #5) (This document sets out the evidence to be relied on)

(b) Joint Affidavit (see Sample #6)

(c) Financial Statement (see Sample #13) (if child or spousal support is to be paid)
or
Waiver of Financial Statements (see Sample #7) (if no support of any kind is to be paid)

(d) Support Deduction Order (Sample #15) (where child and/or spousal support is being paid)

(e) Support Deduction Order Information Form (Sample #16) (where child and/or spousal support is being paid)

(f) Case Information Statement (Sample #17) (only if you are filing for divorce in Toronto, Sault Ste. Marie, or Windsor)

(g) Divorce Judgment (see Sample #8)

(h) Requisition (see Sample #9)

(i) Certificate of Divorce (see Sample #10)

(j) Affidavit (re no appeal) (see Sample #11)

The Joint Affidavit (see Sample #6) must be sworn before a lawyer, notary public, or a commissioner for taking oaths.

3. The Motion Record

Once you have completed these documents, you are ready to form your Motion Record and file your documents with the court. The Motion Record is a collection, in booklet form, of all the documents that have to be filed in the registrar's office. They are put together in chronological order so that the court officials and the judge can refer to them quickly and easily.

The Record must contain typed copies or photocopies of the originals. Photocopies will be allowed only if they are clear and true duplicates. Your record must contain the following documents in the order listed:

(a) A table of contents or index, describing each document by its name and date. This should also give the page number (or tab number if you separate the documents by tabs) of each document in the Record (therefore, you must number all the pages in the Motion Record; see Sample #4).

(b) The Notice of Motion

(c) A *copy* of the Petition for Divorce (You must keep the Petition with the original signatures separated from the bound Record.)

(d) The Waiver of Financial Statements (or Financial Statement if applicable)

(e) The Joint Affidavit

(f) A Record Back (the same as shown in Sample #2 but typed on light blue cardboard or stiff paper that can be purchased at a stationery store or with the set of forms available from the publisher)

Staple the Record together (three staples down the left side of the bundle) to form a neat package (like a book), number the pages consecutively, and list the titles and page numbers of the documents on the contents page. Make an extra copy of the Record, typed or photocopied, to keep for yourself.

4. Filing your documents

After your Motion Record is prepared, take it to your nearest court office along with the original Petition for Divorce, your marriage certificate, four copies of your Divorce Judgment (see Sample #8), and two self-addressed, stamped envelopes: one addressed to you and one addressed to your spouse. These are for the use of the court when it mails the Divorce Judgment to you and your spouse.

If you are not certain that your Record and other documents are in order, ask one of the clerks in the divorce section of the court office to check them over for you. There may be slight differences in the procedure for filing from office to office, but the clerks will be able to assist you and inform you if anything is missing. (Both spouses do *not* have to do this; only one spouse need file the Petition.)

Locate the nearest Ontario Court (General Division) courthouse by referring to the blue pages of your telephone book under Governments, Ontario, Attorney General or by phoning your nearest court building.

You will be required to pay the following fees when you file your forms:*

(a) $135 for a Clearance Certificate (for your marriage certificate "search" by the ministry; the court will provide an individual petitioner with the form to complete for a Clearance Certificate) and for issuing the Petition — cash or by money order made payable to the Minister of Finance.

(b) $170 to "set a joint or uncontested matter down" — cash or by money order made payable to the Minister of Finance.

(c) $18 for your Certificate of Divorce payable to the Minister of Finance.

Pay the filing fee to the cashier. He or she will stamp the date on all copies and "seal" the original Petition. A court clerk will also stamp a number on the upper right-hand corner and will retain the Record for the court file.

5. Application for judgment

If you have filed a Joint Petition for divorce, you and your spouse are applying and are eligible for judgment in the court office *immediately* after the Petition is accepted by the court (i.e., the process described above is completed).

Remember that the court will not give you a Divorce Judgment unless you and your spouse have lived separate and apart for at least one year, but you can process the paperwork ahead of time. The Divorce Judgment will be signed by a judge once you have filed the above documents.

After 31 days from the date the Judgment is signed, you can make application to the registry where the Petition was filed to obtain a Certificate of Divorce. You do this by completing the Requisition (see Sample #9), the draft Certificate of Divorce (see Sample #10), and the Affidavit (see Sample #11). Take these court documents to the court office for signing with your $18 fee (cash or money order made payable to the Minister of Finance). The Certificate is confirmation that your divorce is final.

Note that all fees are subject to change without notice. Please check all fees with the appropriate office before submitting funds.

Court File No.

ONTARIO COURT (GENERAL DIVISION)

BETWEEN:

JOAN PUBLIC

Petitioner (Wife)

-and-

JOHN QUE PUBLIC

Respondent (Husband)

MOTION RECORD

Date: , 199-

JOAN PUBLIC
322 Lakeshore Road
Toronto, Ontario

Court File No.

ONTARIO COURT (GENERAL DIVISION)

BETWEEN:

JOAN PUBLIC

Petitioner (Wife)

-and-

JOHN QUE PUBLIC

Respondent (Husband)

I N D E X

<u>**TAB**</u>

1. Requisition to Note Default and Notice of Motion for Judgment dated August 2, 199-.

2. Petition for Divorce, dated May 2, 199-.

3. Affidavit of the Petitioner, sworn May 2, 199-.

Court file no._____

ONTARIO COURT (GENERAL DIVISION)

BETWEEN:

John Que Public   HUSBAND

- and -

Joan Public   WIFE

NOTICE OF MOTION

The motion is for default judgment in accordance with the petition.

The grounds for the motion are that the spouses jointly petitioned for divorce.

The following documentary evidence will be relied on:

1. the petition

2. the certificate of marriage or the registration of marriage filed in this action

3. the affidavits of the husband and wife petitioner dated ___July 2, 199-___

   (List any other)

~~The petitioners intend to present oral evidence at the hearing of the motion.~~

(Delete if not applicable)

Date ___August 2, 199-___

Names, addresses, and telephone numbers of petitioners.

John Que Public
1000 Yonge Street
Toronto, Ontario
555-1111

Joan Public
322 Lakeshore Road
Toronto, Ontario
555-5666

INTERNATIONAL SELF-COUNSEL PRESS LTD.
1481 Charlotte Road
North Vancouver, B.C. V7J 1H1
DIVONT-JOINT (2-1) 91

Court file no. _____

ONTARIO COURT (GENERAL DIVISION)

BETWEEN:

Type in name of husband.

JOHN QUE PUBLIC   (HUSBAND)

- and -

Type in name of wife.

JOAN PUBLIC   (WIFE)

JOINT AFFIDAVIT

Name of husband   We, _____John Que Public_____ (Husband), of

City, town   the __City of Toronto_____ in the__Municipality of____
Municipality or county
Name of wife   Metropolitan Toronto_____ and _____Joan Public_____ (Wife),

City, town   of the _City of Toronto_____, in the _Municipality of_____
Municipality or county
Metropolitan Toronto_____, MAKE OATH AND SAY AS FOLLOWS:

1. We are the husband and wife described above and as such have knowledge of the matters
   to which we hereinafter depose.

2. We are jointly petitioning for divorce on the grounds that we have lived separate and apart
   since the ____1st_____ day of ____June_____, 199-_____.

3. There is no possibility of our reconciliation. The following efforts to reconcile have taken
   place: None

Set out particulars. If no efforts to reconcile have been made, state "None"

4. The particulars of our marriage as contained in the Certificate of Marriage are true. Attached hereto and marked as Exhibit "A" is a true copy of the Marriage Certificate.

INTERNATIONAL SELF-COUNSEL PRESS LTD.
1481 Charlotte Road
North Vancouver, B.C. V7J 1H1
DIVONT-JOINT (3-1) 92

5. All the information as set out in the Joint Petition for Divorce, filed, that relates to details of the marriage and separation is correct.

Insert the number of children. If there are no children, type in "no."

6. We have _____ no _____ child(ren).

Their names and dates of birth are as follows:

Name   Birthdate

Not applicable

Type in "mother" or "father."

We are the parents of the child(ren). The child(ren) have lived with the _____ since birth and we agree that they should continue to do so.

The child(ren) are currently residing at _____

                                                                    (address)

Type in "mother" or "father" as appropriate.

7. We are in agreement that there should be joint custody where the _____ has access to the child(ren) during the following times:

Set out in detail all access arrangements, exactly as described in Petition.

Not applicable

8. This arrangement is in the best interests of the child(ren) for the following reasons:

Not applicable

INTERNATIONAL SELF-COUNSEL PRESS LTD.
1481 Charlotte Road
North Vancouver, B.C. V7J 1H1
DIVONT-JOINT(3-2) 92

9. The arrangements we have made for support are as follows:

Amount paid   Time period   Paid by   Paid for
                     (weekly, monthly)   (husband or wife)   (name of child)

    Not applicable

10. We have agreed that the support arrangements for the child(ren) should be as set out above based on the financial statements, filed, and the budgets of the children. We agree that the child(ren) cost approximately $_____ per month and, based on our earnings, we agree that the _____ should pay $_____ to the _____.

Type in "father" or "mother" as appropriate.
Type in "father" or "mother" as appropriate.

11. The educational needs of the children are being met.

12. The following are all other court proceedings with reference to the marriage or any child(ren) of the marriage:

Set out particulars. If none, state "None."

    Not applicable

13. We have entered into the following domestic contracts and other written or oral financial arrangements:

Set out particulars. If none, state "None."

    Date   Nature of contract or arrangement   Status

    None

INTERNATIONAL SELF-COUNSEL PRESS LTD.
1481 Charlotte Road
North Vancouver, B.C. V7J 1H1
DIVONT-JOINT(3-3) 92

14. There has been no agreement, conspiracy, understanding or arrangement to which we are directly or indirectly a party for the purpose of subverting the administration of justice, fabricating or suppressing evidence, or deceiving the Court.

15. We have agreed that the issues of property and spousal support have been settled. We do not claim a division of property at this time and we are aware that a claim for a division of property may be barred after the divorce.

16. Neither the husband nor the wife intends to appeal the Divorce Judgment.

17. The present address for the husband is: _1000 Yonge Street, Toronto, Ontario_

    The means by which this is known are: _personal knowledge_

18. The present address for the wife is: _322 Lakeshore Road, Toronto, Ontario_

    This means by which this is known are: _personal knowledge_

SEVERALLY SWORN BEFORE ME at the)
City of Toronto)
in the Municipality of)
Metropolitan Toronto)
this 2nd day of July) *John Q. Public*
19 9- .) John Que Public
)
)
) *Joan Public*
) Joan Public

I. C. Ewe

A Commissioner for taking Affidavits.

INTERNATIONAL SELF-COUNSEL PRESS LTD.
1481 Charlotte Road
North Vancouver, B.C. V7J 1H1
DIVONT-JOINT (3-4) 92

Court file no._____

ONTARIO COURT (GENERAL DIVISION)

BETWEEN:

John Que Public   HUSBAND

- and -

Joan Public   WIFE

WAIVER OF FINANCIAL STATEMENTS

The husband and the wife waive financial statements in respect of claims made in this action for support under the Divorce Act.

Date: _July 2, 199-_ _____   Date: _July 2, 199-_ _____

Joan Public _____   _John Q. Public_ _____
Signature of wife   Signature of husband

Wife's name _Joan Public_ _____   Husband's name _John Que Public_ _____

Address: _322 Lakeshore Road_ ____   Address: _1000 Yonge Street_ _____
     Toronto, Ontario   _Toronto, Ontario_

_Z1P 0G0_ _____   _Z1P 0G0_ _____

Tel. No: _555-5666_ _____   Tel. No: _555-1111_ _____

Court file no._____

ONTARIO COURT (GENERAL DIVISION)

THE HONOURABLE JUSTIN J. JUDGE   Monday August 2   19 9-

(day and date judgment given)

BETWEEN:

JOHN QUE PUBLIC   HUSBAND,

- and -

(Court seal)

JOAN PUBLIC   WIFE

DIVORCE JUDGMENT

THIS MOTION made jointly by the spouses for judgment for divorce was heard this day at ___Toronto, Ontario_____

(place)

The spouses jointly petitioned for divorce.

ON READING the petition, the notice of motion for judgment, the affidavit dated _____July 2, 199-_____ of the husband and the wife

(date)

filed in support of the motion and

(add any other material filed)

INTERNATIONAL SELF-COUNSEL PRESS LTD.
1481 Charlotte Road
North Vancouver, B.C. V7J 1H1
DIVONT-JOINT (7-1) 91

1. THIS COURT ORDERS AND ADJUDGES THAT __John Que Public__

(names of spouses)

and _____Joan Public_____

who were married at ____Toronto, Ontario_____

(place)

on __December 27, 199-_____

(date)

are divorced and that the divorce takes effect on ___August 9, 199-_____

(date)

2. THIS COURT ORDERS AND ADJUDGES

~~This judgment bears interest at the rate of _____ percent per year commencing on~~ _____

(date)

(This clause required in a judgment for the payment of money on which postjudgment interest is payable. Delete if inapplicable.)

If you are claiming support, add the Family Support Plan paragraph here.

Justin J. Judge

(In a judgment that provides for payment of support, set out the last known address of the support creditor and debtor.)

THE SPOUSES ARE NOT FREE TO REMARRY UNTIL THIS JUDGMENT TAKES EFFECT, AT WHICH TIME A CERTIFICATE OF DIVORCE MAY BE OBTAINED FROM THIS COURT. IF AN APPEAL IS TAKEN IT MAY DELAY THE DATE WHEN THIS JUDGMENT TAKES EFFECT.

INTERNATIONAL SELF-COUNSEL PRESS LTD.
1481 Charlotte Road
North Vancouver, B.C. V7J 1H1
DIVONT-JOINT (7-2) 91

Court file no. _____

ONTARIO COURT (GENERAL DIVISION)

BETWEEN:

John Que Public   HUSBAND
(   )

-and-

Joan Que Public   WIFE
(   )

REQUISITION

To the Registrar at the ___Municipality of Metropolitan Toronto___

- I request you to issue a Certificate of Divorce in the above title of proceeding commenced at ___Toronto_____;
- Affidavit attached;
- Copy of Divorce Judgment, as issued, attached/

THIS SECTION FOR OFFICE USE ONLY

I HAVE SEARCHED THE COURT RECORDS PURSUANT TO RULE 70.22 (c) AND HAVE ASCERTAINED THAT THERE IS NO INDICATION THAT THE AFFIDAVIT FILED IS INCORRECT

This _____ day _____ 19 _____

Local Registrar

Per: _____
         Senior Counter Clerk

Date:

Firm Name:

Address:

Tel. No:

SCP-DIVONT-JOINT(12-1)97

Court file no._____

ONTARIO COURT (GENERAL DIVISION)

(Court seal)

CERTIFICATE OF DIVORCE

This is to certify that the marriage of

John Que Public

and

Joan Public

which was solemnized at ___Toronto, Ontario___

on ___December 27, 1984___

was dissolved by a judgment of this court which became effective on ___August 9, 199-___
(date)

Date: ___August 15, 199-___   Issued by:_____
Local registrar

at

INTERNATIONAL SELF-COUNSEL PRESS LTD.
1481 Charlotte Road
North Vancouver, B.C. V7J 1H1
DIVONT-JOINT (8-1) 91

Court file no. _____

ONTARIO COURT (GENERAL DIVISION)

BETWEEN:

John Que Public   HUSBAND
( )

-and-

Joan Que Public   WIFE
( )

AFFIDAVIT

I, _John Que Public_____ , of the _City Of Toronto_____

in the _Municiality of Metropolitan Toronto_____

MAKE OATH AND SAY (or AFFIRM):

1.   I am the Husband/Wife herein and as such have knowledge of the matters hereinafter deposed to.
2.   No appeal from the divorce is pending.
3.   No order has been made extending the time for appealing from the divorce.

SWORN BEFORE ME at the _____)
)
of _____ in the   )
)
_____) _____
)
this ____ day of _____ 19 ____)

_____
A Commissioner for taking Affidavits, etc.

SCP-DIVONT-JOINT(13-1)97

50

d. PREPARATION OF SOLE PETITION

You will note from Sample #12 that when you are applying for a divorce as a sole petitioner, there is a standard Petition for Divorce which can be obtained from the store where you bought this book or from other department, book, and stationery stores. You may also obtain the forms from the publisher by sending in the coupon at the front of this book. Alternatively, you can type the whole Petition yourself.

The publisher's package of forms contains two sets of the form: one set for rough work and one set for the final work.

Refer to Sample #12 when filling out your Petition. Make certain that your name, as petitioner, and your spouse's name, as respondent, are exactly as shown in the marriage certificate. If you or your spouse is known by any other name, show the names as follows:

John Que Public,
otherwise known as
John Que Private

1. Explanatory notes for completing a Sole Petition

Complete all relevant sections of the Petition as briefly and concisely as possible. Refer to the examples that state the best pleadings for your grounds for divorce.

You will note that on the first page of the Petition for Divorce the number of days the other party is allowed to file a defence (called an Answer) must be shown. Your spouse may also counter-petition you or sue you for certain relief. This is called an Answer and Counter-Petition. If your spouse is served in Ontario, he or she is allowed 20 days in which to answer; if your spouse is served in another province or state, he or she is allowed 40 days in which to answer; if he or she is served elsewhere, 60 days are allowed.

When you have completed your Petition, but before you sign it, make one photocopy. Then sign both the original and the copy.

Paragraph 1 — Claim

You must ask the judge for what you want from the court. This "relief" will be in the form of "orders" given by the judge. If you propose to include provisions of a separation agreement in the Divorce Judgment, you should refer to the specific provisions to be included.

The following is a list of the most commonly sought orders:

(a) A divorce

(b) Custody of the infant children of the marriage

(c) Support for the petitioner and the infant children

(d) Costs against the respondent spouse (You should always insert this even though you may have no reasonable expectations of getting it.)

Remember, you must consider exactly what relief you want the court to grant, and ask for it. The court will not, in most circumstances, allow you to add requests for relief at the trial of your divorce action without ordering that the documents be re-served on the respondent.

Paragraph 2 — Grounds

Refer to the section of the act under which you intend to proceed. Make certain you have the full and accurate Divorce Act section number. Check with the section numbers that I have supplied; say exactly what has happened to give rise to this Petition. Additional examples are as follows.

Adultery

The respondent spouse has committed adultery. Particulars are as follows:

Since the date of the marriage, the husband has engaged in adulterous sexual intercourse with one Jane Private on or about the 15th day of April, 199-, at 425 Wellington Avenue, in the city of London, in the Province of Ontario.

or

Since the date of the marriage, the husband has engaged in adulterous sexual intercourse, and in particular, has committed adultery with one Janis Lane and is presently cohabiting with the said Janis Lane as husband and wife at 925 Wellington Avenue in the City of London, in the Province of Ontario. As a result of the aforementioned relationship, the husband has fathered a child, bearing the name Jake Public, born on the 18th day of December, 199-.

Note: The above examples are the type most commonly used under the adultery section. You will, of course, have to alter the details to fit your specific set of facts.

Cruelty

The respondent has treated the petitioner with physical or mental cruelty of such a kind as to render intolerable the continued cohabitation of the spouses. Particulars are as follows:

(a) The husband has been guilty of numerous acts of violence against me, and in particular, assaulted me during the last week of March 199- and the first week of April 199-. The husband has, for the past five years, been a heavy drinker and has continually come home drunk and has physically and verbally abused me causing me serious emotional upset which required a doctor's treatment;

(b) The husband has on frequent occasions threatened to kill me and the infant children;

(c) The husband has an irrational explosive temper and during his outbursts has destroyed my clothing, thrown meals on the floor, ruined our furniture, and hurled ash-trays at me;

(d) Due to the husband's conduct, I have received medical treatment for injuries suffered and am in fear of ever having to live with the husband again.

Note: The above details about the cruelty are only examples of acts of cruelty which may well constitute grounds for divorce. Obviously, there will be other details that you may wish to include. I suggest that you keep it as brief as possible and that you include only those acts of cruelty that are the most obvious.

Paragraphs 3 and 4 — Reconciliation

If no efforts have been made to reconcile, simply indicate this with the word "none."

The clause in the sample Petition (Sample #12) under the heading "Reconciliation" shows one of the more common steps taken by parties attempting reconciliation.

Paragraphs 5 to 17 — Details of marriage

Make sure the information you put in this section conforms exactly to the statistics in the copy of your marriage registration, which by now you will have received from the Registrar of Vital Statistics.

If you are not certain of your spouse's place and date of birth, indicate as specifically as possible the information you do have (e.g., Poland, March 1940).

Paragraphs 18 to 21 — Residence

Residence means the province where you now live (not necessarily permanently). The court says that you must have resided a certain length of time in a province before you are entitled to proceed with a divorce action. This residence time is 12 months and you must have actually lived in Ontario for 12 months immediately preceding the start of your divorce action.

Paragraphs 22 to 28 — Children

All children who are under 16 years of age, or those over 16 but dependent on either spouse due to illness, disability, or other cause, must be listed in the Petition with their places and dates of birth. See the examples of the proposed custody of the children in Sample #12. Refer also to the section on custody in chapter 3.

Paragraph 29 — Other court proceedings

All Petitions for Divorce filed in the Ontario Court (General Division) must contain a paragraph concerning the "joinder of causes" or other proceedings involved. Virtually everyone involved in a do-it-yourself divorce will indicate that this paragraph is "Not Applicable."

Court file no._____

ONTARIO COURT (GENERAL DIVISION)

The parties should be identified in the title of the proceeding as "husband" and "wife" in addition to their designation as "petitioner" and "respondent." The parties may then be referred to in the body of the document as "husband" and "wife."

BETWEEN:

(Court seal)

Joan Public   PETITIONER
(Wife   )

and

John Que Public   RESPONDENT
(Husband   )

PETITION FOR DIVORCE

TO THE RESPONDENT

A LEGAL PROCEEDING FOR DIVORCE HAS BEEN COMMENCED AGAINST YOU by the petitioner. The claim made against you appears on the following pages.

IF YOU WISH TO DEFEND THIS PROCEEDING, you or an Ontario lawyer acting for you must prepare an answer in Form 70D prescribed by the Rules of Civil Procedure, serve it on the petitioner's lawyer(s) or, where the petitioner does not have a lawyer, serve it on the petitioner, and file it, with proof of service, in this court office, WITHIN TWENTY DAYS after this petition is served on you, if you are served in Ontario.

If you are served in another province or territory of Canada or in the United States of America, the period for serving and filing your answer is forty days. If you are served outside Canada and the United States of America, the period is sixty days.

Instead of serving and filing an answer, you may serve and file a notice of intent to defend in Form 70J prescribed by the Rules of Civil Procedure. This will entitle you to ten more days within which to serve and file your answer.

If this petition for divorce contains a claim for support or division of property, you must serve and file a financial statement in Form 70K prescribed by the Rules of Civil Procedure within the time set out above for serving and filing your answer, whether or not you wish to defend this proceeding. If you serve and file an answer, your financial statement must accompany your answer.

IF YOU FAIL TO SERVE AND FILE AN ANSWER, A DIVORCE MAY BE GRANTED IN YOUR ABSENCE AND WITHOUT FURTHER NOTICE TO YOU, JUDGMENT MAY BE GRANTED AGAINST YOU ON ANY OTHER CLAIM IN THIS PETITION AND YOU MAY LOSE YOUR RIGHT TO SUPPORT OR DIVISION OF PROPERTY. IF YOU WISH TO DEFEND THIS PROCEEDING BUT ARE UNABLE TO PAY LEGAL FEES, LEGAL AID MAY BE AVAILABLE TO YOU BY CONTACTING A LOCAL LEGAL AID OFFICE.

NEITHER SPOUSE IS FREE TO REMARRY until a divorce has been granted and has taken effect. Once a divorce has taken effect, you may obtain a certificate of divorce from this court office.

Date _____   Issued by_____

Local registrar

Name and address of each respondent.

To: John Que Public
1000 Yonge Street
Toronto, Ontario
Z1P 0G0

Address of court office
393 University Ave.
Toronto, Ontario
M5G 1E6

INTERNATIONAL SELF-COUNSEL PRESS LTD.
1481 Charlotte Road
North Vancouver, B.C. V7J 1H1
DIVONT-SOLE(1-1)91

CLAIM

1. The petitioner claims:

In this section, state everything you want the court to include in the judgment. If you claim support or a division of property, set out the nature and amount of relief claimed and the amount of support claimed for each dependant. If you want to include provisions of a separation agreement in the judgment, refer to the specific provisions to be included.

(a) a divorce;

(b) Under the Divorce Act,
- (i) interim and permanent custody of the child of the marriage, Robert John Public, born June 1, 1985
- (ii) interim and permanent support for the child, Robert John Public, in the amount of $500 per month
- (iii) costs, including interim disbursements

(c) Under the Family Law Act,
- (i) an order for child support of the child of the marriage, Robert John Public, in the amount of $500 per month
- (ii) an Order that all support payments be increased annually on the anniversary date of the Order by the percentage change in the Consumer Price Index for Canada for all prices of all items since the same month of the previous year as published by Statistics Canada pursuant to section 34(5) and (6) of the Act
- (iii) an Order requiring the respondent to pay proportionately to income the cost of post-secondary education for the child of the marriage
- (iv) equalization of all family property pursuant to section 5 of the Act
- (v) interim and permanent exclusive possession of the matrimonial home at 322 Lakeshore Road, Toronto, Ontario
- (vi) costs, including interim disbursements

If relief is claimed under any other Act, refer to the Act in the claim.

(d) Under the Children's Law Reform Act,
- (i) interim and permanent custody of the child of the marriage, Robert John Public, born June 1, 1985
- (ii) an Order restraining the Respondent from removing the child from the province of Ontario without the consent in writing of the Petitioner, or further Court Order

(e) Under the Change of Name Act,
- (i) an Order that neither party shall change the surname of the child

(f) Under the Courts of Justice Act,
- (i) pre-judgment and post-judgment interest pursuant to sections 138 and 139 of the Act

(g) Costs

INTERNATIONAL SELF-COUNSEL PRESS LTD.
1481 Charlotte Road
North Vancouver, B.C. V7J 1H1
DIVONT-SOLE(1-2) 91

GROUNDS FOR DIVORCE — SEPARATION

2. (a) The spouses have lived separate and apart since ___June 1, 199-___
(Date)

The spouses have resumed cohabitation during the following periods in an unsuccessful attempt at reconciliation:

Date(s) of cohabitation

None

GROUNDS FOR DIVORCE — ADULTERY

2. ~~(b) The respondent spouse has committed adultery. Particulars are as follows:~~

GROUNDS FOR DIVORCE — CRUELTY

2. ~~(c) The respondent has treated the petitioner with physical or mental cruelty of such a kind as to render intolerable the continued cohabitation of the spouses. Particulars are as follows:~~

INTERNATIONAL SELF-COUNSEL PRESS LTD.
1481 Charlotte Road
North Vancouver, B.C. V7J 1H1
DIVONT-SOLE(1-3) 91

RECONCILIATION

State details. If no efforts have been made, state "none."

3. There is no possibility of reconciliation of the spouses.
4. The following efforts to reconcile have been made:

The parties made an effort to reconcile by attending family counselling at the Clarke Institute during the months of February, March, and April 199-.

DETAILS OF MARRIAGE

If possible, copy this information from the marriage certificate.

5. Date of marriage: December 27, 1984

6. Place of marriage: Toronto, Ontario
(City, town, or municipality, province or state, country)

7. Wife's surname immediately before marriage: Jones

8. Wife's surname at birth: Jones

9. Husband's surname immediately before marriage: Public

10. Husband's surname at birth: Public

11. Marital status of husband at time of marriage: Never married
(Never married, divorced, or widower)

12. Marital status of wife at time of marriage: Never married
(Never married, divorced, or widow)

13. Wife's birthplace: Toronto, Ontario
(City, town, or municipality, province or state, country)

14. Wife's birthdate: April 11, 1985

15. Husband's birthplace: Calgary, Alberta
(City, town, or municipality, province or state, country)

16. Husband's birthdate: May 12, 1954

Check one of (a), (b), or (c) and complete.

17. (a) [X] A certificate of [ ] the marriage [X] the registration of the marriage of the spouses has been filed with the court.

(b) [ ] It is impossible to obtain a certificate of the marriage or its registration because:

(c) [ ] A certificate of the marriage or its registration will be filed before this action is set down for trial or a motion is made for judgment.

INTERNATIONAL SELF-COUNSEL PRESS LTD.
1481 Charlotte Road
North Vancouver, B.C. V7J 1H1
DIVONT-SOLE(1-4) 91

RESIDENCE

18. The petitioner has resided in __Toronto, Ontario__
    (City, town, or municipality, and province, state or country)
    since__April 11, 1955__
    (Date)

19. The respondent has resided in __Toronto, Ontario__
    (City, town, or municipality, and province, state or country)
    since__December, 1982__
    (Date)

20. The respondent's current address is__1000 Yonge Street__

Check appropriate box or boxes

21. The [x] petitioner [x] respondent has habitually resided in Ontario for at least one year immediately preceding the commencement of this proceeding.

CHILDREN

22. The following are all the living children of the marriage as defined by the Divorce Act:

Full name	Birthdate	School and grade or year	Person with whom child lives and length of time child has lived there.
Robert John Public	June 1, 1985	The Great School Grade 4	The child has lived with husband and wife since his birth.

The children ordinarily reside in:__Toronto, Ontario__
(City, town, or municipality, and province, state or country)

Make sure that this paragraph agrees with the claim under 1. above.

23. (a) The petitioner seeks an order for custody or joint custody of the following children on the following terms:

Name of child	Terms of the order
Robert John Public	Custody to the wife; liberal and generous access to the husband

Check appropriate box.

The respondent [ ] agrees [x] does not agree with the above terms.

INTERNATIONAL SELF-COUNSEL PRESS LTD.
1481 Charlotte Road
North Vancouver, B.C. V7J 1H1
DIVONT-SOLE(1-5) 91

Strike out if not applicable.

Check appropriate box.

~~(b)   The petitioner is not seeking an order for custody and~~

☐ is content that a previous order for custody remain in force

☐ is attempting to obtain an order for custody in another proceeding full particulars of which are as follows:

State name of court, court file number and particulars of the order or proceeding.

Strike out if not applicable.

~~(c)   The petitioner seeks an order for access (visiting arrangements) and is content~~ ~~that the respondent have an order for custody of the following children on the fol-~~ ~~lowing terms:~~

Name of child   Terms of the order

Check appropriate box.

~~The respondent ☐ agrees   ☐ does not agree with the above terms.~~

INTERNATIONAL SELF-COUNSEL PRESS LTD.
1481 Charlotte Road
North Vancouver, B.C. V7J 1H1
DIVONT-SOLE(1-6) 91

24. (a) The following are the existing visiting arrangements (access) for the spouse who does not have the children living with him or her:

State details such as days of the week, hours of visits, and place of access.

Both spouses continue to occupy the matrimonial home. The wife has, since the date of the separation, assumed the day-to-day care of the child.

INTERNATIONAL SELF-COUNSEL PRESS LTD.
1481 Charlotte Road
North Vancouver, B.C. V7J 1H1
DIVONT-SOLE(1-7) 91

Check appropriate box.

(b) The existing visiting arrangements (access) are ☐ satisfactory ☒ not satisfactory.

If not satisfactory, state reasons and describe how the arrangements should be changed.

The husband has not committed himself to any specific access schedule which makes it difficult for the wife to maintain continuity in her own life as well as that of the child. Although the husband travels a great deal with his profession, he is capable of providing a monthly flight schedule around which access can be arranged.

25.   The order sought in paragraph 23 is in the best interests of the children for the following reasons:

(i) The wife is self-employed as an accountant and works out of the matrimonial home

(ii) Since the child's birth, the wife has been primarily responsible for his care

(iii) The husband's employment as a pilot necessitates him travelling extensively

(iv) The wife and child have a close relationship and it is in the child's best interests to sustain their close bond

(v) The wife is in a better position to meet the day-to-day needs of the child

26.   The following material changes in the circumstances of the spouses are expected to affect the children, their custody and the visiting arrangements (access) in the future:

The wife is claiming exclusive possession of the matrimonial home and the circumstances for the child will not change materially. The wife proposes that the husband have visiting arrangements as his time and schedule permit and is in the best interests of the child.

INTERNATIONAL SELF-COUNSEL PRESS LTD.
1481 Charlotte Road
North Vancouver, B.C. V7J 1H1
DIVONT-SOLE(1-8) 91

27. (a) The existing arrangements between the spouses for support of the children are as follows:

Amount paid	Time period (Weekly, monthly, etc.)	Paid by (Husband or wife)	Paid for (Name of child)

There are no existing arrangements between the spouses for the support of the child.

(b) The existing support arrangements ☐ are being honoured ☐ are not being honoured.

Not applicable

(c) The petitioner proposes that the support arrangements for the children should be as follows:

Amount to be paid	Time period (Weekly, monthly, etc.)	To be paid by (Husband or wife)	To be paid for (Name of child)
Interim $500	monthly	husband	Robert John Public
Permanent $700	monthly	husband	Robert John Public

28. The educational needs of the children ☒ are being met ☐ are not being met.

INTERNATIONAL SELF-COUNSEL PRESS LTD.
1481 Charlotte Road
North Vancouver, B.C. V7J 1H1
DIVONT-SOLE(1-9)91

OTHER COURT PROCEEDINGS

State the name of the court, the court file number, the kind of order the court was asked to make, and what order, if any, the court made. If the proceeding is not yet completed, state its current status.

29. The following are all other court proceedings with reference to the marriage or any child of the marriage:

There have been no other court proceedings with reference to

the marriage. .

DOMESTIC CONTRACTS AND FINANCIAL ARRANGEMENTS

Indicate whether the contract or arrangement is now in effect, and if support payments are not being paid in full, state the amount that has not been paid.

30. The spouses have entered into the following domestic contracts and other written or oral financial arrangements:

Date	Nature of contract or arrangement	Status

There have been no domestic contracts or financial arrangements

between the husband and wife.

COLLUSION, CONDONATION, AND CONNIVANCE

31. There has been no collusion in relation to this divorce proceeding.

Strike out paragraph 32 if the divorce is sought on the ground of separation only.

Where there has been condonation or connivance, strike out the previous sentence. State details and set out the facts relied on to justify a divorce in the circumstances

32. There has been no condonation of or connivance at the grounds for divorce in this proceeding.

INTERNATIONAL SELF-COUNSEL PRESS LTD.
1481 Charlotte Road
North Vancouver, B.C. V7J 1H1
DIVONT-SOLE(1-10) 91

MATTERS OTHER THAN DIVORCE AND CUSTODY

Set out in separate, consecutively numbered paragraphs the material facts relied on to substantiate the claims.

33. The grounds for the relief sought in paragraph 1, other than a divorce or custody, are as follows:

   (i) The wife has filed her Financial Statement along with her Petition for Divorce

   (ii) The wife requires support in the amount of $500.00 per month to meet the needs of the child

   (iii) The husband earns $35,000 a year and is capable of assisting financially in meeting the day-to-day needs of the child

Exclusive Possession of the Matrimonial Home

   (i) The child has resided in the matrimonial home since his birth

   (ii) The wife carries on business out of the matrimonial home

   (iii) The child's school is within walking distance of the matrimonial home

   (iv) The child has established close contacts with the neighbours and has friends with whom he associates daily

Accounting

   (i) The husband and wife own joint and separate assets that require valuation and accounting for the purposes of calculating their net family property

   (ii) The wife claims an equalization of Net Family Property according to section 5 of the Family Law Act

INTERNATIONAL SELF-COUNSEL PRESS LTD.
1481 Charlotte Road
North Vancouver, B.C. V7J 1H1
DIVONT-SOLE(1-11) 91

TRIAL

Where a claim is made for custody of a child who ordinarily resides in Ontario, the place of trial must be in the county where he or she ordinarily resides.

34. The petitioner proposes that if there is a trial in this action, it be held at:

Toronto, Ontario

DECLARATION OF PETITIONER

35. I have read and understand this petition for divorce. The statements in it are true, to the best of my knowledge, information, and belief.

Date___May 2, 199-_____   *Joan Public*_____
                                            (Signature of petitioner)

(Name, address, and telephone number of petitioner)

Joan Public
322 Lakeshore Road
Toronto, Ontario Z1P 0G0
(416) 555-5666

INTERNATIONAL SELF-COUNSEL PRESS LTD.
1481 Charlotte Road
North Vancouver, B.C. V7J 1H1
DIVONT-SOLE(1-12) 81

However, those of you who are bringing a claim against your spouse for a portion of his or her separate property or business assets should briefly state the nature of your claim here, and if you have already had a hearing on the matter, you should also indicate the result of your claim. If the claim was to be joined (heard at the same time) with your Petition, then all of the extra documents in support of this claim will also have to be filed.

In any event, if you are advancing a claim against your spouse's property under the Family Law Act, it is highly unlikely that you are acting without legal representation. You certainly should have such representation.

This section also includes matters such as family court support hearings, previous divorce actions, custody actions, or actions for annulment. If you were involved in any such proceedings, simply indicate when the matter was heard and the result. If there is a previous action still not completed, consult a lawyer so that it can be disposed of.

Paragraph 30 — Domestic contracts and financial arrangements

Simply state the date of any pertinent agreements, either written or oral.

Paragraph 31 and 32 — Collusion, condonation, and connivance

If you are guilty of collusion, your divorce will be refused. If you are guilty of condonation or connivance, your Petition will be dismissed unless the judge feels it would be in the public interest to grant the divorce.

Collusion is an agreement to manufacture, fabricate, or suppress evidence in order to deceive the court and secure a divorce.

Condonation means that you forgave your spouse for the acts that you are now using as grounds for divorce. Condonation actually arises if you continue to live with your spouse or return to live with him or her after learning of his or her misconduct. Remember,

however, if you have lived with your spouse for a period or periods not more than 90 days after learning of his or her misconduct in an attempt to effect a reconciliation, you will not be guilty of condonation.

Connivance means that you either encouraged your spouse's conduct or stood idly by and did nothing about it.

If you feel you may have a problem complying with these requirements, you should consult a lawyer.

Paragraph 32 concerning condonation and connivance is not relevant if the divorce is sought on the ground of separation only.

Paragraph 33 — Matters other than divorce and custody

Here you set out the details in support of claims other than for the divorce itself and custody of any children. As shown in the sample, these details would normally relate to a claim for support.

Paragraph 34 — Trial

If your divorce action will be going to trial, you will appear before a judge.

2. Financial statement

If you are asking for child or spousal support or division of assets, both spouses will have to file a Financial Statement, as shown in Sample #13. You must attach to the Financial Statement a copy of your most recent tax return and tax assessment notice.

To get your spouse to fill out the appropriate form, send a Notice to File Financial Statement (see Sample #14). Your spouse must file this form within the same time limits for filing an Answer to the Petition. (The time limits are noted on the first page of the Petition.)

3. Support Deduction Order and Support Deduction Order Information Form

Under the Family Support Plan Act, all matters involving custody and/or support must include a Support Deduction Order and a Support Deduction Order Information Form. You should file these with your Petition (see Samples #15 and #16).

The Support Deduction Order and the Information Form are reviewed and signed by a judge. The employer is then ordered to deduct monthly support payments from the payor spouse's wages. These payments are forwarded to the Family Support Plan and then to the recipient.

Follow these steps to fill out the Support Deduction Order:

(a) Fill in the name of court as "Ontario Court (General Division)" and give the address of the courthouse where you are filing the petition, e.g., "393 University Avenue, Toronto."

(b) Fill in the court file number and names of petitioner and respondent. Do not fill in the date; the court will insert this information.

(c) In paragraph 1, fill in the name of the person who will be paying support.

(d) File the Support Deduction Order with your Motion Record after serving your spouse with the Petition.

Follow these steps to fill out the Support Deduction Order Information Form:

(a) Fill in the name of court as "Ontario Court (General Division)" and give the address of the courthouse where you are filing the Petition.

(b) Under "TYPE OF SUPPORT ORDER," put an X in the box next to "FINAL."

(c) Fill in the court file number.

(d) Fill in which Family Support Plan Regional Office you fall under (see the blue pages of your phone book) and your case number, if you know it.

(e) Complete sections 1. and 2. Check off "Additional income source..." if the payor has more than one source of income, i.e., two jobs. Check off "Payor not receiving..." if the payor

is self-employed or is otherwise not capable of paying through payroll deduction because there is no employer/employee relationship. Check off "Recipient does not know" if you do not know the payor's place of employment.

(f) Complete section 3., leaving shaded areas blank.

(g) Fill in your name next to "Prepared by."

(h) File the Support Deduction Order Information Form with your Motion Record after serving your spouse with the Petition.

4. Case Information Statement

You must complete the Case Information Statement only if you are filing for divorce in the cities of Toronto, Sault Ste. Marie, and Windsor (see Sample #17). Case management is a system employed by the courts whereby a judge is assigned to monitor your case to ensure that it is resolved efficiently. This means that one judge is appointed to hear all matters on the case arising from the litigation until trial. This should not be a concern for you if you are expecting to obtain an uncontested divorce. You will receive a Case Management Timetable when you issue your Petition, which will set deadlines for filing of materials. Follow the deadlines given and you will have no difficulty.

Follow these steps to fill out the Case Information Statement:

(a) Fill in the court office address and the title of the case, e.g., "Public v. Public."

(b) Under "THIS FORM FILED BY," put an X in the box next to "applicant/petitioner/plaintiff."

(c) Under "ORDER SOUGHT...," put an X in the box next to "divorce" and indicate any other orders you are seeking.

(d) Complete "PERSON FILING THIS FORM," "OTHER SPOUSE," and

"CHILDREN" sections with the information requested.

(e) Under "THIS PERSON'S LAWYER," provide your own name, address, and telephone number. Fill in the date.

(f) File the Case Information Statement along with your Petition.

5. Filing the documents

You may commence the proceedings in any district except, as has been stated earlier, if you and your spouse reside in Hamilton, London, Barrie, Kingston, and/or Napanee. However, if custody and/or access of the children is involved, the trial (if one is necessary) must take place in the county or district where the child resides.

Take your filing fee, your marriage certificate (or copy of your marriage certificate), and your documents (including your original Petition and the signed copy) to the Ontario Court (General Division). Have the official in charge of divorce matters look through your documents to see that they are in order.

Pay the filing fee to the cashier; he or she will stamp the date on the file copy and process a copy through the cash register. This indicates to the court officials that you have, in fact, paid the necessary fee. (Currently, the fee is $135 which must be made in cash or money order payable to the Minister of Finance. This includes $125 for issuing the Petition and $10 for the clearance certificate. Personal cheques are not accepted.)

Return the documents to the official at the divorce counter. He or she will date and sign the Petition for Divorce, assign a number to your action, and then stamp the Ontario Court (General Division) seal on the original Petition. The registrar retains the copy with the cash register stamp and you receive back the original. You must then photocopy the required number of copies for service on the respondent and the co-respondent (if applicable).

You will need the original and two copies of the Petition for Divorce if one party only is to be served and there are no infant children; you will need the original and three copies if two people are to be served and there are no infant children. If there are infant children and only one party to be served, you will need three copies. If there are infant children and two parties to be served, you will need the original and four copies.

You are now ready to have the Petition and Financial Statement (if applicable) served on the appropriate parties.

6. Serving the documents

You must serve the documents within six months of filing them with the registrar. Unless there is a court order to the contrary, you must have the Petition for Divorce served on your spouse and on any other person named in the divorce proceedings either in the Title of Proceedings or in the body of the Petition. If you are basing your Petition on adultery, the person against whom adultery is alleged need be served only if he or she is named in the Petition. If you have been given a Case Management Timetable by the court, this must also be served on the respondent.

The Notice to File the Financial Statement and your Financial Statement must also be served on your spouse, if Financial Statements are necessary. Service of Financial Statements is required if the Petition contains a claim for support or division of property. In response to the claim, the respondent must serve and file Financial Statements. Automatic filing of Financial Statements where a claim for custody is made is no longer required.

Court file no. _____

ONTARIO COURT (GENERAL DIVISION)

BETWEEN:

Joan Public   PETITIONER, (Wife   )

- and -

John Que Public   RESPONDENT (Husband   )

FINANCIAL STATEMENT

I, __Joan Public_____ of the __City_____
           (full name of deponent)   (city, town, etc.)

of __Toronto_____ in the __Municipality_____
                                      (county, municipality, etc.)

of __Metropolitan Toronto_____ make oath and say:
                                         /affirm:

1. Particulars of my financial situation and of all my property are accurately set out below, to the best of my knowledge, information, and belief.

ALL INCOME AND MONEY RECEIVED

(Include all income and other money received from all sources, whether taxable or not. Show gross amount here and show deductions on pages 2, 3, 4 & 5. Give current actual amount where known or ascertainable. Where amount cannot be ascertained, give your best estimate. Use weekly, monthly or yearly column as appropriate.)

Category	Weekly	Monthly	Yearly
1. Salary or wages			$35,000.00
2. Bonuses			
3. Fees			
4. Commissions			
5. Family allowance		$33.93	
6. Unemployment insurance			
7. Workers' compensation			
8. Public assistance			
9. Pension			
10. Dividends			
11. Interest			
12. Rental income			
13. Allowances and support from others			
14. Other (Specify)			
TOTAL	$	(A)$ 33.93	$35,000.00

Weekly total $_____ × 4.33 = (B)$_____ monthly

Yearly total $ __35,000.00__ ÷ 12 = (C)$ __2916.66__ monthly

GROSS MONTHLY INCOME (A) + (B) + (C) = (D)$ __2950.59__

INTERNATIONAL SELF-COUNSEL PRESS LTD.
1481 Charlotte Road
North Vancouver, B.C. V7J 1H1
DIVONT-SOLE (2-1) 91

OTHER BENEFITS

(Show all non-monetary benefits from all sources, such as use of a vehicle or room and board, and include such items as insurance or dental plans or other expenses paid on your behalf. Give your best estimate where you cannot ascertain the actual value.)

Item	Particulars	Monthly Market Value

TOTAL (E) $ 2,950.59

GROSS MONTHLY INCOME AND BENEFITS (D) + (E)=$ _____

ACTUAL AND PROPOSED BUDGETS

CATEGORY	ACTUAL BUDGET for twelve month period from June 1 ____, 199– to June 1 ____, 199– Show actual expenses, or your best estimate where you cannot ascertain actual amount.			PROPOSED BUDGET Show your proposed budget, giving your best estimate where you cannot ascertain actual amount.		
	Weekly	Monthly	Yearly	Weekly	Monthly	Yearly
Housing 1. Rent		$1,000		1.		
2. Real property taxes				2.		$1,200
3. Mortgage				3.	$1,000	
4. Common expense charges				4.		
5. Water		$15		5.	$15	
6. Electricity		$20		6.	$20	
7. Natural gas		$100		7.	$100	
8. Fuel oil				8.		
9. Telephone		$25		9.	$25	
10. Cable T.V.		$20		10.	$20	
11. Home insurance			$600	11.		$600
12. Repairs and maintenance			$100	12.		$100
13. Gardening and snow removal				13.		
14. Other (Specify)				14.		
Food, Toiletries and Sundries 15. Groceries	$50			15. $75		
16. Meals outside home	$10			16. $20		
17. Toiletries and sundries	$20			17. $25		
18. Grooming	$20			18. $30		

INTERNATIONAL SELF-COUNSEL PRESS LTD.
1481 Charlotte Road
North Vancouver, B.C. V7J 1H1
DIVONT-SOLE (2-2) 91

CATEGORY	ACTUAL BUDGET			PROPOSED BUDGET		
Food Toiletries and Sundries–cont'd.	Weekly	Monthly	Yearly	Weekly	Monthly	Yearly
19. General household supplies	$20			19. $25		
20. Laundry, dry cleaning	$10			20. $20		
21. Other (Specify)				21.		
Clothing		$100				
22. Children				22.	$200	
23. Self		$100		23.	$200	
Transportation						
24. Public transit		$150		24.	$150	
25. Taxis, car pools	$10			25. $20		
26. Car Insurance			$450	26.		$450
27. Licence			$70	27.		$70
28. Car maintenance			$500	28.		$500
29. Gasoline, oil	$20			29.		
30. Parking	$5			30.		
31. Other (Specify)				31.		
Health and Medical						
32. Doctors, chiropractors				32.		
33. Dentist (regular care)			$120	33.		$200
34. Orthodontist or special dental care				34.		$1,000
35. Insurance premiums			$720	35.		$720
36. Drugs				36.		
37. Other (Specify)				37.		
Deductions from Income						
38. Income tax		$500		38.		$500
39. Canada Pension Plan		$30		39.		$30
40. Unemployment insurance		$30		40.		$30
41. Employer pension				41.		
42. Union or other dues				42.		

INTERNATIONAL SELF-COUNSEL PRESS LTD.
1481 Charlotte Road
North Vancouver, B.C. V7J 1H1
DIVONT-SOLE (2-3) 91

CATEGORY	ACTUAL BUDGET			PROPOSED BUDGET		
Deductions from Income—cont'd.	Weekly	Monthly	Yearly	Weekly	Monthly	Yearly
43. Group insurance				43.		
44. Credit union loan				44.		
45. Credit union savings				45.		
46. Other (Specify)				46.		
Miscellaneous						
47. Life insurance premiums			$200	47.		$200
48. Tuition fees, books, etc.				48.		
49. Entertainment	$10			49. $20		
50. Recreation	$10			50. $20		
51. Vacation			0	51.		$500
52. Gifts			0	52.		$500
53. Babysitting, day care	$50			53. $75		
54. Children's allowances				54.		
55. Children's activities	$10			55. $20		
56. Support payments				56.		
57. Newspapers, periodicals		$10		57.	$10	
58. Alcohol, tobacco		$50		58.	$75	
59. Charities				59.		
60. Income tax (not deducted at source)				60.		
61. Other (Specify)				61.		
Loan Payments						
62. Banks				62.		
63. Finance companies				63.		
64. Credit unions				64.		
65. Department stores				65.		
66. Other (Specify)				66.		

INTERNATIONAL SELF-COUNSEL PRESS LTD.
1481 Charlotte Road
North Vancouver, B.C. V7J 1H1
DIVONT-SOLE (2-4) 91

CATEGORY	ACTUAL BUDGET			PROPOSED BUDGET		
	Weekly	Monthly	Yearly	Weekly	Monthly	Yearly
Savings						
67. R.R.S.P.				67.		
68. Other (Specify)				68.		
	$	$	$	$	$	$

TOTALS OF ACTUAL BUDGET

Monthly Total $ 2,150.00

Weekly Total $ 245   × 4.33 = $ 1,060.85

Yearly Total $ 2,760.00   ÷ 12 = $ 230.00

MONTHLY ACTUAL BUDGET   = (F) $ 3,440.85

TOTALS OF PROPOSED BUDGET

Monthly Total $ 2,375.00

Weekly Total $ 380.00   × 4.33 = $ 1,645.00

Yearly Total $ 6,040.00   ÷ 12 = $ 503.55

MONTHLY PROPOSED BUDGET   = (G) $ 4,523.95

SUMMARY OF INCOME AND EXPENSES

Actual

Gross monthly income
(Amount D from page 1) $ 2,950.59

Subtract Monthly actual budget
(Amount F from page 5)   − $ 3,440.85

ACTUAL MONTHLY SURPLUS / DEFICIT $ 490.26

Proposed

Gross monthly income
(Amount D from page 1) $ 2,950.59

Subtract Proposed monthly budget
(Amount G from page 5)   − $ 4,523.95

PROPOSED MONTHLY SURPLUS / DEFICIT $ 1,573.36

INTERNATIONAL SELF-COUNSEL PRESS LTD.
1481 Charlotte Road
North Vancouver, B.C. V7J 1H1
DIVONT-SOLE (2-5) 91

LAND

(Include any interest in land owned on the valuation date, including leasehold interests and mortgages, whether or not you are registered as owner. Include claims to an interest in land, but do not include claims that you are making against your spouse in this or a related proceeding. Show estimated market value of your interest without deducting encumbrances or costs of disposition, and show encumbrances and costs of disposition under Debts and Other Liabilities on page 9.)

Nature and Type of Ownership State percentage interest where relevant.	Nature and Address of Property	Estimated Market Value of Your Interest as of: See instructions above.		
		Date of Marriage	Valuation Date	Date of Statement
Joint tenancy 50%	Matrimonial home, 322 Lakeshore Road Toronto, Ontario	125,000.00	135,000.000	$140,000.00
TOTAL $		62,500.00	(H)67,500.00	$70,000.00

GENERAL HOUSEHOLD ITEMS AND VEHICLES

(Show estimated market value, not cost of replacement for these items owned on the valuation date. Do not deduct encumbrances here, but show encumbrances under Debts and Other Liabilities on page 9.)

Item	Particulars	Estimated Market Value of Your Interest as of: See instructions above.		
		Date of Marriage	Valuation Date	Date of Statement
General household contents excluding special items (a) at matrimonial home(s)	Refrigerator, stove, washer, dryer, furniture, etc.	$10,000.00	8,000.00	5,000.00
(b) elsewhere Jewellery	Diamond ring (gift)	1,000.00	1,200.00	1,400.00
Works of art Vehicles and boats	1984 Station wagon	15,000.00	13,000.00	10,000.00
Other special items				
TOTAL $		26,000.00	(I)22,200.00	16,400.00

INTERNATIONAL SELF-COUNSEL PRESS LTD.
1481 Charlotte Road
North Vancouver, B.C. V7J 1H1
DIVONT-SOLE (2-6) 91

SAVINGS AND SAVINGS PLANS

(Show items owned on the valuation date by category. Include cash, accounts in financial institutions, registered retirement or other savings plans, deposit receipts, pensions and any other savings.)

Category	Institution	Account Number	Amount as of:		
			Date of Marriage	Valuation Date	Date of Statement
None					
		TOTAL $		(J)	

SECURITIES

(Show items owned on the valuation date by category. Include shares, bonds, warrants, options, debentures, notes and any other securities. Give your best estimate of market value if the items were to be sold on an open market.)

Category	Number	Description	Estimated Market Value as of:		
			Date of Marriage	Valuation Date	Date of Statement
None					
		TOTAL $		(K)	

LIFE AND DISABILITY INSURANCE

(List all policies owned on the valuation date.)

Company and Policy No.	Kind of Policy	Owner	Beneficiary	Face Amount	Cash Surrender Value as of:		
					Date of Marriage	Valuation Date	Date of Statement
INS Co.	Life	Self	Child	$100,000	no cash surrender value		
				TOTAL $		(L)	

INTERNATIONAL SELF-COUNSEL PRESS LTD.
1481 Charlotte Road
North Vancouver, B.C. V7J 1H1
DIVONT-SOLE (2-7) 91

ACCOUNTS RECEIVABLE

(Give particulars of all debts owing to you on the valuation date, whether arising from business or from personal dealings.)

Particulars	Amount as of:		
	Date of Marriage	Valuation Date	Date of Statement
None			
TOTAL $		(M)	

BUSINESS INTERESTS

(Show any interest in an unincorporated business owned on the valuation date. A controlling interest in an incorporated business may be shown here or under Securities on page 7. Give your best estimate of market value if the business were to be sold on an open market.)

Name of Firm or Company	Interest	Estimated Market Value as of:		
		Date of Marriage	Valuation Date	Date of Statement
None				
	TOTAL $		(N)	

OTHER PROPERTY

(Show other property owned on the valuation date by categories. Include property of any kind not shown above. Give your best estimate of market value.)

Category	Particulars	Estimated Market Value as of:		
		Date of Marriage	Valuation Date	Date of Statement
None				
	TOTAL $		(O)	

INTERNATIONAL SELF-COUNSEL PRESS LTD.
1481 Charlotte Road
North Vancouver, B.C. V7J 1H1
DIVONT-SOLE (2-8) 91

DEBTS AND OTHER LIABILITIES

(Show your debts and other liabilities on the valuation date, whether arising from personal or business dealings, by category such as mortgages, charges, liens, notes, credit cards and accounts payable. Include contingent liabilities such as guarantees and indicate they are contingent.)

Category	Particulars	Amount as of:		
		Date of Marriage	Valuation Date	Date of Statement
None				
	TOTAL $		(P)	

PROPERTY, DEBTS AND OTHER LIABILITIES ON DATE OF MARRIAGE

(Show by category the value of your property and your debts and other liabilities calculated as of the date of your marriage. Do not include the value of a matrimonial home that you owned at the date of marriage.)

Category	Particulars	Value as of date of marriage	
		Assets	Liabilities
None			
	TOTAL $	(Q) $	(R) $

NET VALUE OF PROPERTY OWNED ON DATE OF MARRIAGE (Amount Q Subtract Amount R) = (S) $_____

INTERNATIONAL SELF-COUNSEL PRESS LTD.
1481 Charlotte Road
North Vancouver, B.C. V7J 1H1
DIVONT-SOLE (2-9) 91

EXCLUDED PROPERTY

(Show the value by category of property owned on the valuation date that is excluded from the definition of "net family property".)

Category	Particulars	Value on Valuation Date
Gift	Diamond ring	$1,200.00
	TOTAL	(T) $1,200.00

DISPOSAL OF PROPERTY

(Show the value by category of all property that you disposed of during the two years immediately preceding the making of this statement, or during the marriage, whichever period is shorter.)

Category	Particulars	Value
	TOTAL	(U) $

INTERNATIONAL SELF-COUNSEL PRESS LTD.
1481 Charlotte Road
North Vancouver, B.C. V7J 1H1
DIVONT-SOLE (2-10) 91

CALCULATION OF NET FAMILY PROPERTY

Value of all property owned on valuation date (Amounts H,I,J,K,L,M,N and O from pages 6 to 8) $ 89,700.00

Subtract value of all deductions (Amounts P and S from page 9)   — $ _____

Subtract value of all excluded property (Amount T from page 10)   — $ 1,200.00

               NET FAMILY PROPERTY $ 88,500.00

2. The name(s) and address(es) of my employer(s) are:

3. Attached to this affidavit are a copy of my income tax return filed with the Department of National Revenue for the last taxation year, together with all material filed with it, and a copy of any notice of assessment or reassessment that I have received from the Department for that year.

4. I do not anticipate any material changes in the information set out above.

(Delete inapplicable paragraph 4)

4. ~~I anticipate the following material changes in the information set out above:~~

(Give particulars:)

Sworn before me at the City of Toronto
Affirmed

in the Municipality of Metropolitan
     Toronto

                               Joan Public

on   July 2,   19 9-   *Signature of deponent*

     Commissioner for Taking Affidavits, etc.

INTERNATIONAL SELF-COUNSEL PRESS LTD.
1481 Charlotte Road
North Vancouver, B.C. V7J 1H1
DIVONT-SOLE (2-11) 91

Court file no._____

ONTARIO COURT (GENERAL DIVISION)

BETWEEN:

Joan Public   PETITIONER

(Wife   )

- and -

(Court seal)

John Que Public   RESPONDENT

(Husband   )

NOTICE TO FILE FINANCIAL STATEMENT

TO: John Que Public

In this proceeding a claim has been made against you for_____support_____

_____

YOU ARE REQUIRED, WHETHER OR NOT YOU DEFEND THIS PROCEEDING, to serve and file a financial statement in Form 70N prescribed by the Rules of Civil Procedure. Your financial statement must accompany your responding document if you defend this proceeding and must be served and filed in any event within the time for delivering your responding document after the original process in this proceeding was served on you.

If you fail to file a financial statement as required, an order may be made without further notice to compel you to file a financial statement.

_____

Date

Joan Public

322 Lakeshore Road

Toronto, Ontario Z1P 0G0

555-5666

Petitioner appearing in person

To:

John Que Public

1000 Yonge Street

Toronto, Ontario Z1P 0G0

_____

INTERNATIONAL SELF-COUNSEL PRESS LTD.
1481 Charlotte Road
North Vancouver, B.C. V7J 1H1
DIVONT-SOLE (3-1) 91

SAMPLE #15
SUPPORT DEDUCTION ORDER

Name of Court <u>Ontario Court (General Division)</u>
Nom du tribunal

SUPPORT DEDUCTION ORDER
ORDONNANCE DE RETENUE DES ALIMENTS

Location <u>393 University Avenue, Toronto, Ontario</u>
Lieu

Family Support Plan Act
Loi sur le Régime des obligations alimentaires envers la famille

Form/*Formule 1*

Court file no./*Nº de dossier du tribunal*

_____
Judge/*Juge*

_____
Date

Between:/*Entre:*

JOAN PUBLIC

~~Applicant~~/Petitioner/~~Plaintiff~~
Requérant/Demandeur

and / *et*

JOHN QUE PUBLIC

Respondent/Defendant
Intimé/Défendeur

SUPPORT DEDUCTION ORDER / *ORDONNANCE DE RETENUE DES ALIMENTS*

Upon making an order this day which provides for payment of support on a periodic basis at regular intervals and on
Après avoir rendu une ordonnance ce jour qui prévoit le versement d'aliments sur une base périodique à intervalles réguliers et après

making the necessary inquiries required by section 3.1(3) of the Family Support Plan Act:
avoir fait les recherches nécessaires visées au paragraphe 3.1(3) de la Loi sur le Régime des obligations alimentaires envers la famille:

1.   THIS COURT ORDERS THAT <u>John Que Public</u> pay support as set out in
LE TRIBUNAL ORDONNE que   *verse les aliments tel qu'il*

the attached information form.
est énoncé dans la formule de renseignements ci-jointe.

2.   THIS COURT ORDERS that any income source that receives notice of this support deduction order make
LE TRIBUNAL ORDONNE que toute source de revenu qui reçoit avis de la présente ordonnance fasse des

payments to the Director of the Family Support Plan in respect of the payor out of money owed by the
versements au directeur du Régime des obligations alimentaires envers la famille à l'égard du payeur à même l'argent

income source to the payor.
que la source de revenu doit au payeur.

_____
Signature of Judge, Registrar, or Clerk of the Court
Signature du juge, ou du greffier du tribunal

SELF-COUNSEL PRESS LTD.
1481 Charlotte Road
North Vancouver, B.C. V7J 1H1
DIVONT SOLE (11-1) 93

SAMPLE #16
SUPPORT DEDUCTION ORDER INFORMATION FORM

Name of Court __Ontario Court (General Division)__

Location __393 University Avenue, Toronto, Ontario__

SUPPORT DEDUCTION ORDER INFORMATION FORM
Family Support Plan Act

Note: Please print.
Leave shaded areas blank,
the court will fill them in.

Type of Support Order
Interim ☐ Final ☐

Form 2

Court file no.

FAMILY SUPPORT PLAN (F.S.P.) FILE INFORMATION
Family Support Plan Regional Office _____

F.S.P. Case Number (if known) | | | | | | |

1. INFORMATION ON PARTIES

Payor name __John Que Public__ Birthdate | 1 | 2 | 0 | 5 | 5 | 4 | Sex ☒ M ☐ F
Day Month Year

Payor address __1000 Yonge Street, Toronto, Ontario Z1P OGO__
Street and Number   Town/City   Province   Postal code

Recipient name __Joan Public__ Birthdate | 1 | 0 | 0 | 4 | 5 | 5 | Sex ☐ M ☒ F
Day Month Year

Payor address __322 Lakeshore Road, Toronto, Ontario Z1P OGO__
Street and Number   Town/City   Province   Postal code

2. INFORMATION ON PAYOR'S EMPLOYER(S) AND OTHER INCOME SOURCE(S)

Employer/Income source name __FlyBy Airline Co.__ Telephone __555-2345__

Payroll office address __100 Airport Road Malton   Ontario   Z1P OGO__
Street and number   Town/City   Province   Postal code

☐ Additional income source information attached.
☐ Payor not receiving periodic payments as explained in the Family Support Plan Act.
☐ Recipient does not know.

3. SUPPORT ORDER INFORMATION

The attached support deduction order relates to a support order which says that:

__John Que Public__ is required to pay support for the following persons:
Payor name

(Court will change this list if necessary)

NAME	BIRTHDATE DAY MONTH YEAR	AMOUNT PAYABLE	FREQUENCY OF PAYMENTS	PAYMENTS TO BEGIN DAY MONTH YEAR
Spouse a.	/ /	$		/ /
Other Dependants b. Robert John	01 / 06 / 85	$		/ /
c.	/ /	$		/ /
d.	/ /	$		/ /
e.	/ /	$		/ /

Is the support order a variation of a previous support order? ☐ Yes ☒ No

4. COST OF LIVING ADJUSTMENTS ☐ None provided

Support is indexed in accordance with ☐ s.34(5) of the Family Law Act OR ☐ as per attached OR
☐ as follows _____

5. ARREARS (Complete if applicable)

Arrears are fixed at $_____ as of the _____ day of _____ 19____

To be paid as follows (if applicable): _____

6. TERMINATION OF SUPPORT (Complete if previously ordered support is terminated by this order)

Support is terminated for the following persons
for _____ on the _____ day of _____ 19____
for _____ on the _____ day of _____ 19____

Prepared by __Joan Public__

SELF-COUNSEL PRESS LTD.
1481 Charlotte Road
North Vancouver, B.C. V7J 1H1
DIVONT SOLE (12-1) 93

CASE INFORMATION STATEMENT

Form 1   COURT FILE NO: _____

Courts of Justice Act

ONTARIO COURT (GENERAL DIVISION)

SHORT TITLE OF CASE   Public   -and-   Public
_____

CASE INFORMATION STATEMENT

THIS FORM FILED BY

[X]   applicant/petitioner/plaintiff   [ ] other - specify kind and party and give name
[ ]   respondent/defendant - give name

ORDER SOUGHT BY PERSON FILING THIS FORM

Divorce Act	Family Law Act	Children's Law Reform Act	Other
[X] divorce	[X] child support	[X] [X] custody	[ ] constructive/resulting trust
[X] child support	[ ] spousal support	[ ] access	[ ] partition/sale
[ ] spousal support	[X] property - equalize	[ ] paternity declaration	[ ] annulment
[X] custody	[X] excl. possession	[ ] other - specify	[ ] other - specify
[ ] access	[ ] restraining order		
[ ] other - specify	[ ] other - specify		

PERSON FILING THIS FORM

[X] married - date   Dec. 27, 1984   Separated - date   June 1, 1996
[ ] not married -
    cohabited from - date   Separated - date

Birth date   April 11, 1958   Social Insurance Number   441 321 337
Employer's name,
address and
telephone

OTHER SPOUSE

Birth date   May 12, 1954   Social Insurance Number   441 532 182
Employer's name,   Airline Company, 1 Main Street
address and   Toronto, Ontario Z1P 0G0
telephone   (416) 555-4444

CHILDREN   Name and birth date   Name and birth date

Robert John Public, Born June 1, 1985 ....

THIS PERSON'S LAWYER (if no lawyer, give person's name, address for service, telephone and fax numbers)

Name and firm   Joan Public
Address   322 Lakeshore Road, Toronto, Ontario Z1P 0G0
Telephone   Fax   Date
(416) 555-5666   January 29, 1997

SCP-DIVONT SOLE (12-1)97

82

Where a claim for division of property is made in a Petition for Divorce, a Net Family Property Statement (see Sample #18) must be filed seven days before a pretrial conference, a motion for judgment, or the trial.

You can serve the respondent by mail with an Acknowledgment of Receipt Card (see Sample #19) by personal service, or through your spouse's lawyer if the lawyer agrees to accept service. You can also enlist the services of the sheriff of the county in which your spouse resides. This method is useful if you expect your spouse to be unco-operative.

The following is a more detailed description of methods of service, beginning with the easiest.

(a) Service by mail

The Petition for Divorce can be served on your spouse and any other person by mailing the appropriate documents to the last known address of the person to be served. But service by mail is effective only if the Acknowledgment of Receipt Card (see Sample #19) or a post office receipt bearing the signature of the person served is received by the sender.

Once the card is sent back, the sender must produce an affidavit of service for the court, attaching the card that verifies receipt by the respondent. The affidavit is filed when you go to set the divorce down at court. The affidavit should indicate the date the card was sent, to which address it was sent, and when it was received back. Attach the card to the affidavit.

If your spouse is unco-operative, and you think he or she will refuse to sign the Acknowledgment of Receipt Card, you shouldn't use this method to serve your documents.

(b) Service on a lawyer

Service on someone who has a lawyer may be made by leaving a copy of the document with the lawyer or an employee in the lawyer's office. But service in this way is effective only if the lawyer endorses on the documents (or a copy of them) an acceptance of service and the date of acceptance.

(c) Personal service

Your spouse can be personally served by having someone leave a copy of the document with him or her and having your spouse sign the Acknowledgment of Service on the backing sheet of the Petition for Divorce (see Sample #20). Please note that you personally cannot serve any person who may be named in the Petition for Divorce. Some other person must effect personal service.

(d) Service by sheriff

It may be that you cannot serve your spouse by mail and your spouse does not have a lawyer. It may also be that you do not know anyone who can serve your spouse personally. In this case, the documents can be served by the sheriff of the county in which your spouse resides. If your spouse is located in some isolated area, the sheriff, whose office is also located in the courthouse, will instruct you on how best to serve him or her.

You must take all your documents and copies to the sheriff. In addition, you should make sure you have some money with you so that you are in a position to give a deposit against the sheriff's fees.

The sheriff serving the documents must swear an affidavit to confirm to the court that those persons with an actual interest in the proceedings have been notified that you are proceeding with an action for divorce.

The standard Affidavit of Service simply says that a certain person served the documents on the spouse and party with whom adultery has been alleged (if applicable) at a certain time and place (see Sample #21). A separate Affidavit of Service must be completed for each person served.

If you think your spouse will avoid service, be prepared to supply the sheriff with as much information as possible regarding his or her habits, place of work, etc.

If possible, the endorsement on the Petition backing sheet should be properly signed and witnessed. If it is not, the Affidavit of Service should provide an explanation.

A copy of the Petition is attached to the sheriff's affidavit and marked as "Exhibit A."

(e) Service by sheriff outside your county

If the party or parties to be served live outside your county, the sheriff in the county where the parties live may serve the documents. If this is your case, follow these steps:

(a) Obtain the address of the appropriate sheriff's office from your local sheriff.

(b) Go in person to the sheriff's office. If this is not possible, prepare a letter of instruction for the sheriff that lists the addresses of the parties to be served (preferably both home and business); your spouse's (and the co-respondent's) telephone number, if available; and a picture of your spouse and the other person to be served (if possible).

(c) Enclose two or three copies of the Petition for Divorce (as the case may be): one copy for the respondent, one copy for the other person (if applicable), and one copy for the sheriff to affix to the Affidavit of Service.

(d) Enclose copies of the Financial Statement and Notice to File Financial Statement.

The sheriff may wish his or her fee secured, and the terms must be satisfied (e.g., prepayment or deposit). I suggest that you prepare a letter similar to the one shown in Sample #22 if you intend to instruct the sheriff by letter.

If you do not have a photograph of your spouse, instruct the sheriff to establish identification by the best means available. In some cases, the respondent and/or the person with whom adultery has been alleged will permit the serving officer to take a photograph. In other cases, the sheriff's officer will be able to obtain sufficient information, along with the signature acknowledging receipt of the documents, to satisfy the court requirements for identification. In some cases, the party (or parties) will give the sheriff's officer a photograph to be used in the Affidavit of Service.

If you require the sheriff's officer to serve any other party named in the Petition, you must supply the address of that person's residence, place of business, etc. A picture of the other party may also be helpful.

It is important to remember that the sheriff's office will prepare the Affidavit of Service as part of its service and will give you the affidavit once the amount is paid.

It will cost a minimum of $25 to have the documents served by a sheriff's officer. This varies, of course, according to the distance the officer has to travel and how many trips he or she must make to serve the documents. However, if you send a deposit in the amount of $20 or $25 along with your letter enclosing the documents, any unused portion of your deposit will be refunded when the Affidavit of Service is sent to you.

(f) Service by process server

If you do not have a picture of your spouse, I suggest you hire a private process server who may wish to establish identity by taking a picture of your spouse at the time of service. The process server will require the same documents and information as the sheriff.

If you do engage a process server, you will have to prepare the Affidavit of Service to be sworn by him or her. The process server will provide you with the particulars of service and, when the affidavit is prepared, will take it to a notary public or a commissioner for taking affidavits and have it sworn. This affidavit should be included in the fee.

(g) Service by substitution

If you do not know the whereabouts of your spouse, you will require what is known as an "Order for Substituted Service." In other words, if your spouse cannot be served personally with the Petition for Divorce, the court must order that you be allowed to serve the Petition in some other manner, such as publishing a notice in a newspaper or posting documents in an appropriate registry.

In many cases, the petitioner simply does not know where the spouse is, either because they have been separated for a considerable length of time, or because the spouse is effectively covering his or her tracks to avoid creditors or certain financial obligations to the family.

In such circumstances, the petitioner is obviously going to have difficulty serving the documents. As a court appearance and preparation of fairly complicated documentation is required to obtain an order for substitutional service; you should retain a lawyer for this purpose only. However, you can still save a good deal in lawyer's fees if you are prepared to extend the following efforts to locate your spouse. (If you don't do these things, you will have to pay a lawyer to do them.)

(a) If you have been separated from your spouse for a long time, write to his or her relatives requesting information about his or her whereabouts. (If you have lost track of your spouse, you might also check the central Divorce Registry in case he or she has already arranged a divorce.)

(b) Place an advertisement in a newspaper published and circulated in the last place your spouse is known to have lived requesting information about his or her whereabouts. Keep in mind that the fees for legal advertisements in newspapers are often very expensive; they can be more than $250.

(c) It may be possible, if your spouse has had difficulties with the law, to contact the police department in the area where he or she was last known to be, requesting any information they can give about his or her whereabouts. You may find, however, that in most instances, the police department does not wish to become involved in civil matters.

(d) Contact friends and acquaintances of your spouse who might be able to give you information about when and where they last saw him or her.

(e) You may also use the services of a credit bureau or collection agency that can do a "skip trace" on your spouse and perhaps uncover his or her whereabouts.

7. Dispensing with service on a person named in the Petition

If you are not able to have your documents served because you have not been able to locate your spouse and/or anyone else named in the Petition, you can obtain a court order dispensing with service on that person. Again, if such an order is necessary, you should retain the services of a lawyer for this purpose only.

8. Role of the Office of the Children's Lawyer

The Office of the Children's Lawyer — formerly the Official Guardian — is charged with the responsibility of protecting the interests of children involved in matrimonial proceedings. The definition of a child is someone under the age of 16 or over the age of 16 who is still dependent on the parents. The only time the Office of the Children's Lawyer becomes involved in a divorce proceeding is when there is a dispute and the court orders that a Children's Lawyer be appointed, or if, during a motion of interim relief, the court considers that a report from the Children's Lawyer would be beneficial. If a Children's Lawyer is appointed in your case, it would be wise for you to consult a lawyer.

Sample #23 shows an Affidavit of Service used to send a copy of the Children's Lawyer's report by mail to your spouse, if your situation comes to this. This affidavit must be sworn by a lawyer or notary public (for which there is a small charge), and it will be included in your court record.

9. How the action is set down for trial

After you have served everyone with all the documents, you must wait the prescribed amount of time shown on the Petition for Divorce (i.e., 20 days if served in Ontario, 40 days if served in another province or state, 60 days if served elsewhere in the world). When the time has expired, you will be required to file the following documents with the court clerk:

(a) The original Petition for Divorce with the Affidavit of Service attached

(b) A Motion Record

(c) Two self-addressed, stamped envelopes — one addressed to you and one addressed to the respondent — for the use of the court when it mails the Divorce Judgment to you and the respondent

(d) Support Deduction Order (Sample #15) (where child and/or spousal support is being paid)

(e) Support Deduction Order Information Form (Sample #16) (where child and/or spousal support is being paid)

(f) Case Information Statement (Sample #17) (only if you are filing for divorce in Toronto, Sault Ste. Marie, or Windsor)

(g) Four copies of the Divorce Judgment (see Sample #24)

(a) Petition for Divorce

You will file the original Petition for Divorce with the Affidavit of Service attached. When the Petition for Divorce is served, whoever serves it will ask the respondent to sign the Petition backing sheet in the space provided (see Sample #20). The respondent is not required to sign the Petition.

Whoever serves the Divorce Petition will then provide the Affidavit of Service (discussed earlier) that states that the respondent was asked to sign the back of the Petition and either signed it or refused to sign and that a copy was left with the respondent at his or her address or place of business.

(b) The Motion Record

The Motion Record is a collection, in booklet form, of all the documents that have to be filed in the registrar's office. They are put together in chronological order so that the court officials and the judge can refer to them quickly and easily. As noted above, the Motion Record is filed at the end of the time allocated on the Petition for Divorce for an Answer (i.e., 20 days if served in Ontario, etc.)

The Record must contain typed copies or photocopies of the originals. Photocopies will be allowed only if they are clear duplicates. Your record must contain the following documents in the order listed:

(a) A table of contents or index, describing each document by its name and date. This should also give the page number (or tab number if you separate the documents by tabs) of each document in the Record (therefore, you must number all the pages in the Motion Record; see Sample #4).

SAMPLE #18
NET FAMILY PROPERTY STATEMENT

Court file no._____

ONTARIO COURT (GENERAL DIVISION)

BETWEEN:

Joan Public

PETITIONER

(Wife)

(Court seal)

and

John Que Public

RESPONDENT

(Husband)

.....Wife's..................................... **NET FAMILY PROPERTY STATEMENT**

Wife's or Husband's

Valuation date...June 1, 199-............ Statement date...August 1, 199-..........

(Complete columns for both husband and wife, showing your assets, debts, etc. and those of your spouse.)

1. VALUE OF ASSETS OWNED ON VALUATION DATE
   (a) Land

Nature and Type of Ownership State percentage interest where relevant.	Nature and Address of Property	Estimated Market Value on valuation date	
		Husband	Wife
Joint tenancy 50%	Matrimonial home, 322 Lakeshore Road Toronto, Ontario	$67,500.00	$67,500.00
	TOTAL (a) $	67,500.00	67,500.00

INTERNATIONAL SELF-COUNSEL PRESS LTD.
1481 Charlotte Road
North Vancouver, B.C. V7J 1H1
DIVONT-SOLE (4-1) 91

(b) General Household Items and Vehicles

Item	Particulars	Estimated Market Value on Valuation Date	
		Husband	Wife
General household contents excluding special items			
(a) at matrimonial home(s)	Refrigerator, stove, washer, dryer, furniture, etc.	4,000.00	4,000.00
(b) elsewhere			
Jewellery	Diamond ring (gift)		1,200.00
Works of art			
Vehicles and boats	1984 Station wagon	6,500.00	6,500.00
Other special items			
TOTAL (b) $		10,500.00	11,700.00

(c) Savings and Savings Plans

Category	Institution	Account Number	Amount on Valuation Date	
			Husband	Wife
		TOTAL (c) $		

INTERNATIONAL SELF-COUNSEL PRESS LTD.
1481 Charlotte Road
North Vancouver, B.C. V7J 1H1
DIVONT-SOLE (4-2) 91

(d) Securities

Category	Number	Description	Estimated Market Value on Valuation Date	
			Husband	Wife
None				
		TOTAL (d) $		

(e) Life and Disability Insurance

Company and Policy No.	Kind of Policy	Owner	Beneficiary	Face Amount	Cash Surrender Value on Valuation Date	
					Husband	Wife
INS Co.	Life	Wife	Child	$100,000	no cash surrender value	
				TOTAL (e) $		

(f) Accounts Receivable

Particulars	Amount on Valuation Date	
	Husband	Wife
None		
TOTAL (f) $		

INTERNATIONAL SELF-COUNSEL PRESS LTD.
1481 Charlotte Road
North Vancouver, B.C. V7J 1H1
DIVONT-SOLE (4-3) 91

(g) Business Interests

Name of Firm or Company	Interest	Estimated Market Value on Valuation Date	
		Husband	Wife
None			
	TOTAL (g) $		

(h) Other Property

Category	Particulars	Estimated Market Value on Valuation Date	
		Husband	Wife
None			
	TOTAL (h) $		

Total value of assets owned on valuation date	TOTAL 1. (Sum of a, b, c, d, e, f, g, h) $		

2. VALUE OF DEBTS AND OTHER LIABILITIES ON VALUATION DATE

Item	Value of debts and other liabilities on Valuation Date	
	Husband	Wife
None		
TOTAL 2. $		

INTERNATIONAL SELF-COUNSEL PRESS LTD.
1481 Charlotte Road
North Vancouver, B.C. V7J 1H1
DIVONT-SOLE (4-4) 91

3. NET VALUE OF PROPERTY, OTHER THAN A MATRIMONIAL HOME, OWNED ON DATE OF MARRIAGE

Item	Husband	Wife
a) Land		
b) General household items and vehicles		
c) Savings and savings plans, pensions		
d) Securities		
e) Life and disability insurance		
f) Accounts receivable		
g) Business interests		
h) Other Property		
TOTAL 3. $		

4. VALUE OF PROPERTY EXCLUDED UNDER SUBS. 4(2) OF THE *FAMILY LAW ACT*

Item	Husband	Wife
1. Gift or inheritance from third person		
2. Income from property expressly excluded by donor or testator		
3. Damages and settlements for personal injuries, etc.		
4. Life insurance proceeds		
5. Traced property		
6. Excluded property by spousal agreement		
7. Other excluded property		
TOTAL 4. $		

5. NET FAMILY PROPERTY (TOTAL 1 MINUS TOTALS 2, 3 and 4)

	Husband	Wife
TOTAL $	78,000.00	79,200.00

Name, address and telephone number of solicitor or party:

Joan Public
322 Lakeshore Road
Toronto, Ontario Z1P 0G0
555-5666

INTERNATIONAL SELF-COUNSEL PRESS LTD.
1481 Charlotte Road
North Vancouver, B.C. V7J 1H1
DIVONT-SOLE (4-5) 91

Court file no. _____

ONTARIO COURT (GENERAL DIVISION)

BETWEEN:

JOAN PUBLIC   PETITIONER
                         (Wife   )

- and -

(Court seal)

JOHN QUE PUBLIC   RESPONDENT
                         (Husband   )

ACKNOWLEDGMENT OF RECEIPT CARD

TO:

You are served by mail with the document enclosed with this card in accordance with the Rules of Civil Procedure.

You are requested to sign the acknowledgment below and mail this card immediately after you receive it. If you fail to do so, the documents may be served on you in another manner and you may have to pay the costs of service.

ACKNOWLEDGMENT OF RECEIPT

I ACKNOWLEDGE that I have received a copy of the following documents:

Petition

Case Information Statement

Timetable/warning

Dated ___August 3, 199-_____ at ___Toronto, Ontario_____

_____

Signature of person served

INTERNATIONAL SELF-COUNSEL PRESS LTD.
1481 Charlotte Road
North Vancouver, B.C., V7J 1H1
DIVONT-SOLE (5-1) 93

SAMPLE #20
BACKING SHEET OF PETITION FOR DIVORCE

RESPONDENT ( )

Court file no. _____

ONTARIO COURT
(GENERAL DIVISION)

Proceedings commenced at

Petition for Divorce

Name, address, and telephone number of petitioner.

Petitioner appearing in person

and

PETITIONER ( )

(Short title of proceeding)

ACKNOWLEDGMENT OF SERVICE

I, _____ am the respondent named in this petition. I acknowledge receipt of a copy of this petition. My address for service of documents in this divorce proceeding is

Date _____

_____
Signature of respondent

_____
Signature of witness

I, _____ served this petition personally on the respondent.

☐ The respondent completed and signed the acknowledgment of service above in my presence and I signed it as witness.

or

☐ The respondent declined to complete and sign the acknowledgment of service.

_____
Signature

Court file no._____

ONTARIO COURT (GENERAL DIVISION)

BETWEEN:

Joan Public   PETITIONER,
                                              (Wife   )

- and -

John Que Public   RESPONDENT
                                              (Husband   )

AFFIDAVIT OF SERVICE

I, ___Fred F. Friend_____ of the City

of ___Toronto_____, in the Municipality

of ___Metropolitan Toronto_____ MAKE OATH AND SAY (or AFFIRM):

1. On ___June 10, 199-_____, I served the respondent,

   ___John Que Public_____ with the ___Petition for Divorce_____

   by leaving a copy with him/her at ___1000 Yonge Street, Toronto, Ontario___ .

2. I was able to identify the person by means of ___his oral confirmation that he was___

   ___the person to be served._____ .

3. I requested the respondent to sign the back of the ___Petition for Divorce___

   and the respondent did (or did not) comply with my request.

SWORN BEFORE ME at the City of   )
___Toronto_____   )
)
in the Municipality of   )
___Metropolitan Toronto_____   )
this _3rd_ day of_July, 199-___   )   ___Fred F. Friend_____
)   *(name)*
_____   )

___J M Commissioner_____

A Commissioner for taking Affidavits, etc.

INTERNATIONAL SELF-COUNSEL PRESS LTD.
1481 Charlotte Road
North Vancouver, B.C., V7J 1H1
DIVONT-SOLE (8-1) 91

Joan Public
322 Lakeshore Road
Toronto, Ontario
Z1P 0G0

June 15, 199-

The Sheriff
The Courthouse
Toronto, Ontario

Dear Sheriff:

Public v. Public — Divorce Proceedings

I am acting on my own behalf in divorce proceedings against my husband. I enclose two [or three] copies of the Petition for Divorce with the request that you serve the documents on my spouse [and on the co-respondent]. Also enclosed is a picture of my husband [and of the other party] to assist your identifying the person[s] to be served.

The following particulars may be of assistance to you.

Name of spouse:	John Que Public
Residence:	1000 Yonge Street, Toronto, Ontario
Place of business:	Ontario Hydro, Toronto, Ontario
Telephone numbers:	555-0000 (home) 555-1111 (business)

I also enclose my cheque for $25 as a deposit against your fees for this service. The balance, if any, of your fees will be remitted immediately upon receipt of your account.

Should you require any further information, please contact me by telephone at 555-5666.

Yours very truly,

Joan Public

Joan Public

Court file no._____

ONTARIO COURT (GENERAL DIVISION)

BETWEEN:

PETITIONER,

Joan Public
(Wife)

- and -

John Public

RESPONDENT

(Husband)

AFFIDAVIT OF SERVICE (By mail)

I, ____Joan Public_____ of the
City_____ of __Toronto_____ in the Municipality___
of Metropolitan Toronto____ MAKE OATH AND SAY (or AFFIRM):

1. On _January 1, 1997_____ , I sent to
the Respondent by regular letter (or registered mail) to _1000 Yonge____
Street, Toronto_____a copy of the Petition for Divorce, and

2. On _January 15, 1997____, I received the attached acknowledgment
of receipt card (or post office receipt) bearing a signature that purports to
be the signature of _____.

SWORN BEFORE ME at the _____)
of _____)
in the _____)
_____)
this ____ day of_____) _____
_____) *(name)*

_____
A Commissioner for taking Affidavits, etc.

SCP-DIVONT-SOLE (7-1) 97

Court file no._____

ONTARIO COURT (GENERAL DIVISION)

THE HONOURABLE Justin J. Judge, Mon. Aug. 2 19 9-_____
(day and date judgment given)

BETWEEN:

Joan Petitioner   PETITIONER,

(Wife   )

- and -

(Court seal)

John Queb Public   RESPONDENT

(Husband   )

DIVORCE JUDGMENT

THIS MOTION made by the petitioner for judgment for divorce was heard this day at_Toronto, Ontario_____
(place)
The respondent did not defend this action although properly served with the petition as appears from the affidavit of service filed.

ON READING the petition, the notice of motion for judgment, the affidavit dated _May 2, 199-_____of the petitioner filed in support of the motion.
(date)
(Add any other material filed.)

SCP-DIVONT-SOLE (10-1) 97

1. THIS COURT ORDERS AND ADJUDGES THAT ___Joan Public___
   (names of spouses)

   and ___John Que Public___

   who were married at ___Toronto, Ontario___
   (place)

   on ___December 27, 1984___
   (date)

   are divorced and that the divorce takes effect on ___August 9, 199-___
   (date)

2. THIS COURT ORDERS AND ADJUDGES

   Under the Divorce Act that:

   1. Custody of the child of the marriage, Robert John Public, born June 1, 1985, be granted to the Petitioner, Joan Public, with reasonable access by the Respondent, John Que Public.
   2. Support to the child of the marriage, Robert John Public, in the amount of $500 per month to be paid by the Respondent, John Que Public, to the Petitioner, Joan Public.

   Under the Family Law Act that:

   3. The Petitioner, Joan Public, be granted exclusive possession of the matrimonial home until 199- when the matrimonial home will be sold and the proceeds distributed equally between the Petitioner and the Respondent.
   4. $_____ shall be paid to the Petitioner as equalization of all Net Family Property.
   5. Costs as between the Petitioner and the Respondent, fixed at $_____.

If you are claiming support, add the Family Support Plan paragraph here.

*THIS COURT ORDERS AND ADJUDGES THAT unless the support order is withdrawn from the Office of the Family Support Plan, it shall be enforced by the Family Support Plan and amounts owing under the support order shall be paid to the Family Support Plan, which shall pay them to the person to whom they are owed.

4. This judgment bears interest at the rate of _____ percent per year on any payment or payments in respect of which there is a default from the date of default.

(This clause required in a judgment for the payment of money on which postjudgment interest is payable. Delete if inapplicable.)

If you are claiming support, add the Family Support Plan paragraph here.

Justin J. Judge

(In a judgment that provides for payment of support, set out the last known address of the support creditor and debtor.) * *

THE SPOUSES ARE NOT FREE TO REMARRY UNTIL THIS JUDGMENT TAKES EFFECT, AT WHICH TIME A CERTIFICATE OF DIVORCE MAY BE OBTAINED FROM THIS COURT. IF AN APPEAL IS TAKEN IT MAY DELAY THE DATE WHEN THIS JUDGMENT TAKES EFFECT.

SCP-DIVONT-SOLE (10-2) 94

*Include this paragraph if you are claiming support.
**If you are claiming support, attach a sheet with the names and addresses of both parties (creditor and debtor).

(b) The Requisition/Notice of Motion (see Sample #25). (This document sets out the evidence to be relied on and should also set out whether or not the petitioner intends to present oral evidence at the hearing, otherwise the matter will proceed by way of affidavit evidence.)

(c) A *copy* of the Petition for Divorce (You must keep the Petition with the original signatures separated from the bound Record.)

(d) The Financial Statement, if applicable

(e) If you have obtained an Order for Substituted Service, a copy of that Order

(f) If you have an Order dispensing with service on a person named in the Petition, a copy of that Order

(g) A copy of any other Order regarding the hearing of the divorce

(h) The Affidavit of the petitioner

(i) The Affidavit of the respondent (if you have one)

(j) Record Back (the same as Sample #2 but typed on light blue cardboard or stiff paper that can be purchased at a stationery store or included with the set of forms available from the publisher)

Staple the Record together (three staples down the left side of the bundle) to form a neat package (like a book), number the pages consecutively, and list the titles and page numbers of the documents on the contents page. Make an extra copy of the Record, typed or photocopied, to keep for yourself.

If you have not already filed the Support Deduction Order and the Support Deduction Order Information Form, you can do so with the Motion.

Wait about three to four weeks for your Record to be processed. You may then phone the registrar's office to ask for the timing on your Divorce Judgment or your trial date. In cases where the evidence presented by Affidavit does not comply with the rules, is insufficient, or is incorrect, the trial judge may require a court hearing. Claims for custody, support, or division of assets, other than on consent, will also, in all likelihood, be sent to trial.

(c) Affidavit evidence

You must file affidavits to be used as evidence. You should file a Petitioner's Affidavit (see Sample #26) and a Respondent's Affidavit (see Samples #27 and #28) or any affidavit of corroborating evidence.

Sample #26 shows a Petitioner's Affidavit in a simple divorce. Use the following checklist to ensure you include all necessary information on your affidavit. Besides filling out clauses 1 and 2, the Petitioner's Affidavit must do the following:

(a) Refer to the certificate or registration of marriage by title, date, and place of issue and the name and office of the person who issued it and state that it contains the correct particulars of the marriage. (If no certificate or registration of marriage has been filed, you must state what efforts have been made to obtain a certificate and why it is impossible, the date and place of marriage, and sufficient particulars to prove the marriage.)

(b) Set out the particulars of the grounds for divorce.

(c) State that there has been no agreement, conspiracy, understanding, or arrangement to which you are a party for the purpose of subverting the administration of justice, fabricating or suppressing evidence, or deceiving the court.

(d) If you are relying on the respondent's adultery or cruelty, state that you have not condoned or connived the act or conduct complained of, or if there has been condonation or connivance, state why it would be in the public interest to grant the divorce.

(e) Provide particulars of the present and proposed custody and access arrangements for each child of the marriage if different than that stated in the Petition.

(f) If you are claiming support, provide particulars of your own and your children's needs and the respondent's means by referring to the Financial Statements filed, and state any change in circumstances since the Financial Statements were filed.

(g) If you do not claim a division of property, state this and that you are aware that a claim may be barred after the divorce.

(h) If you wish to include in the judgment provisions of a consent, settlement, separation agreement, or previous court order, refer to the document as an exhibit and refer to the specific provisions included.

(i) If you are claiming costs, set out the facts to enable the court to decide whether they should be awarded.

(j) If you wish your divorce to take effect earlier than 31 days after the Divorce Judgment is granted, set out the special circumstances to justify why.

(k) Provide the respondent's last known address and state the means by which the address is known.

(d) Divorce Judgment

You must file four copies of a draft Divorce Judgment (see Sample #24) together with stamped, addressed envelopes for each of the parties and the Children's Lawyer, if one is involved. If you, as the Petitioner, chose to appear before a judge to present evidence, rather than presenting affidavit evidence, you should insert the clause "and on hearing the evidence presented by the petitioner" to the last line of the Divorce Judgment.

If the Judgment is granted according to the draft filed, the registrar signs and enters the Judgment and mails a copy of it in the envelopes provided. If the Judgment is to be granted, but not in accordance with the draft filed, the judge will make an endorsement on the Record and will grant the Judgment as of the date when the draft is corrected to conform to the judge's endorsement and filed with the registrar. The registrar will then sign and enter the Judgment and mail it. (The 31-day period for the granting of the Certificate of Divorce begins to run only after the Judgment is granted. A defective draft Judgment will, therefore, delay the finality of the divorce.)

When you have all of these documents in order, you take them to the courthouse. The clerk will search the file and determine whether an Answer has been filed by the respondent. If the respondent has not contested the divorce, the clerk will take your documents. The charge for filing these documents, a process called "setting the matter down," is currently $170, which must be paid in cash or by money order made payable to the Minister of Finance. If an Answer has been filed, then you are going to have a contested divorce that will require a hearing before a judge. This will cost $268 to set down and you should consult a lawyer immediately.

If you are not certain that your Record and other documents are in order, ask one of the clerks in the divorce section of the registrar's office to check them over for you. There may be slight differences in the procedure for filing from office to office, but the clerks will be able to assist you and inform you if anything is missing.

After your documents have been accepted by the clerk, it will take approximately three to four weeks for you to hear anything. The documents are given to a judge to look over and if all the documents are in order, the judge will sign the Divorce Judgment. You will receive a copy in the self-addressed, stamped envelope you provided to the clerk. The respondent will also receive a copy. If the judge finds anything wrong in the documents you submitted, the clerk will call you and let you know what the problem is so that you can correct it.

e. CERTIFICATE OF DIVORCE

After you have received your Divorce Judgment back from the court, wait 31 days. Then fill in the Requisition (Sample #29), your Certificate of Divorce (Sample #9) and the Affidavit (re no appeal) (Sample #30), which tells the court that there has been no appeal from the Judgment. Take these three documents to the courthouse where the clerk will issue your Certificate of Divorce for a fee of $18 payable to the Minister of Finance.

A Certificate of Divorce is legal throughout Canada. For enforcement purposes, it may be registered with any court in a province and enforced in the same manner as if it were an order of that court.

Under the registration section, in Ontario, an order from another province may be registered by filing a certified copy with the local registrar at Toronto; the order will then be entered as an order of the Ontario court. A certified copy of the order may be filed by simply mailing it with a written request that registration is sought pursuant to section 20(3)(a) of the Divorce Act.

f. UNDERTAKING NOT TO APPEAL

The effective date of the final Divorce Judgment can be shortened if there are special circumstances and the spouses agree and undertake that no appeal from the Judgment will be made (see Sample #31). The details demonstrating the special circumstances in support of an expedited Certificate of Divorce should be set out in an affidavit and in your Divorce Judgment.

Examples of such circumstances would be an impending remarriage of one party or the birth of a child.

Therefore, at the same time as the action is set down for trial, you can file the Notice of Motion for Judgment, draft Divorce Judgment, Undertaking Not to Appeal, and Certificate of Divorce.

g. CONDUCT OF THE TRIAL (if one is necessary)

Most uncontested divorces are done over the counter without parties appearing in court. If a trial is required, the results of your work (good or bad) will come under the critical eye of the judge.

My experience has indicated that in cases where the work has been done carefully and thoroughly, the judge will co-operate to the fullest and "take you by the hand" through the proceedings. However, when the judge detects mistakes, omissions, or general sloppy work, he or she will be less helpful. IT IS THEREFORE CRUCIAL THAT ALL YOUR DOCUMENTS BE IN PROPER ORDER AND THAT YOU COMPLETE PROPERLY ALL THE STEPS LEADING UP TO TRIAL.

As mentioned previously, the court appearance is understandably the most difficult part for the layperson. Consider the possibility of retaining a lawyer just to handle your case in court. This could cost you approximately $600. For this fee, a lawyer will also prepare and file the Divorce Judgment. The choice is up to you.

For those who have the confidence and feel they can represent themselves as well as a lawyer can, or for those who simply cannot afford to retain a lawyer, the following detailed explanation of the courtroom procedure will guide you.

The important thing here (besides having your documents in good order) is to watch a session or two of uncontested divorce cases, preferably before the same

Court file no._____

ONTARIO COURT (GENERAL DIVISION)

BETWEEN:

Joan Public   **PETITIONER**
(Wife   )

- and -

(Court seal)

John Que Public   **RESPONDENT**
(Husband   )

REQUISITION

TO THE REGISTRAR:

I require you to note the respondent   John Que Public
(name)
in default in this action on the ground that he/she has not filed an answer within the prescribed time. The petition has been filed with proof of service.

NOTICE OF MOTION

The motion is for default judgment in accordance with the petition.

The grounds for the motion are that the respondent has not filed an answer and has been noted in default.

The following documentary evidence will be relied on:

1. the petition

2. the certificate of marriage or of the registration of marriage filed in this action

3. the affidavit of the petitioner dated   May 2, 199-

(List any other)

4. The Affidavit of the Respondent dated May 2, 199-

~~The petitioner intends to present oral evidence at the hearing of the motion.~~
(Delete if not applicable)

Date   July 15, 199-

Name, address and telephone number of petitioner.

Joan Public

322 Lakeshore Road
Toronto, Ontario Z1P 0G0
555-5666

INTERNATIONAL SELF-COUNSEL PRESS LTD.
1481 Charlotte Road
North Vancouver, B.C. V7J 1H1
DIVONT-SOLE (8-1) 91

Court file no._____

ONTARIO COURT (GENERAL DIVISION)

BETWEEN:

Joan Public   **PETITIONER**

(Wife   )

- and -

(Court seal)   John Que Public

RESPONDENT

(Husband   )

AFFIDAVIT

I,_____ Joan Public _____

of the ____City_____ of ____Toronto_____ , in

the ____Municipality____ *City, town* of ____Metropolitan Toronto_____ ,
          County, Regional Municipality

the petitioner in this action,

MAKE OATH/AFFIRM AND SAY:

1. There is no possibility of the reconciliation of the spouses because: *(Give particulars)*

OR

1. It would clearly not be appropriate in the circumstances for the court to consider the possibility of the reconciliation of the spouses because: *(Give particulars)*

the respondent and I have been living separate and apart since
June 1, 199-

INTERNATIONAL SELF-COUNSEL PRESS LTD.
1481 Charlotte Road
North Vancouver, B.C. V7J 1H1
DIVONT-SOLE (9-1) 91

2. All the information in the petition in this action is correct, with the following exceptions:

(Give particulars. If no exceptions, state "None.")

3. The certificate of marriage No. Z10101 issued December 27, 1984 at Toronto, Ontario and signed by John Doe of the United Church of Canada contains the correct particulars of the marriage.

4. The ground for divorce as stated in the Petition for Divorce is marriage breakdown evidenced by a separation of more than one year.

5. There has been no agreement, conspiracy, understanding, or arrangement to which I am either directly or indirectly a party for the purpose of subverting the administration of justice, fabricating or suppressing evidence or deceiving the court.

6. I do not claim a division of property at this time and I am aware that a claim for a division of property may be barred after the divorce.

7. The Respondent's last known address, as evidenced by the Affidavit of Service, is 1000 Yonge Street, Toronto, Ontario Z1P 0G0.

SWORN BEFORE ME AT
the City of Toronto   )
)
in the Municipality of   )
Metropolitan Toronto   )
this __2nd__ day of __May__ 19__9-__   ) ___*Joan Public*___
         Q M Commissioner   Petitioner's signature

A Commissioner for taking Affidavits, etc.

INTERNATIONAL SELF-COUNSEL PRESS LTD.
1481 Charlotte Road
North Vancouver, B.C. V7J 1H1
DIVONT-SOLE (9-2) 91

Court file no._____

ONTARIO COURT (GENERAL DIVISION)

BETWEEN:

Joan Public   PETITIONER

(Wife   )

- and -

(Court seal)

John Que Public   RESPONDENT

(Husband   )

AFFIDAVIT

I, _____John Que Public_____

of the ____City_____ of ____Toronto_____ , in
        City, town
the ___Municipality_____ of ___Metropolitan Toronto_____ ,
      County, Regional Municipality
the petitioner in this action,

MAKE OATH/AFFIRM AND SAY:

1. There is no possibility of the reconciliation of the spouses because: *(Give particulars)*

OR

1. It would clearly not be appropriate in the circumstances for the court to consider the possibility of the reconciliation of the spouses because: *(Give particulars)*

The Petitioner and I have been living separate and apart since
June 1, 199-.

105

2. All the information in the petition in this action is correct, with the following exceptions:

    (Give particulars. If no exceptions, state "None.")

    None

<table>
<tr><td>SWORN BEFORE ME AT
the City of Toronto</td><td>)</td><td></td></tr>
<tr><td></td><td>)</td><td></td></tr>
<tr><td>in the Municipality of
Metropolitan Toronto</td><td>)</td><td></td></tr>
<tr><td></td><td>)</td><td></td></tr>
<tr><td>this <u>2nd</u> day of <u>May</u> 19<u>9-</u></td><td>)</td><td><u>John Que Public</u></td></tr>
<tr><td><u>ΩM Commissioner</u></td><td></td><td>~~Petitioner's signature~~
Respondent's signature</td></tr>
<tr><td>A Commissioner for taking Affidavits, etc.</td><td></td><td></td></tr>
</table>

Court file no._____

ONTARIO COURT (GENERAL DIVISION)

BETWEEN:

Joan Public **PETITIONER**
(Wife)

- and -

(Court seal)

John Que Public **RESPONDENT**
(Husband)

AFFIDAVIT

I, ___John Que Public_____

of the ___City_____ of ___Toronto_____ , in
the ___Municipality_____ of ___Metropolitan Toronto_____ ,
City, town *County, Regional Municipality*
the petitioner in this action,

MAKE OATH/AFFIRM AND SAY:

1. There is no possibility of the reconciliation of the spouses because: *(Give particulars)*

OR

1. It would clearly not be appropriate in the circumstances for the court to consider the possibility of the reconciliation of the spouses because: *(Give particulars)*

The Petitioner and I have been living separate and apart since
June 1, 199-.

107

2. All the information in the petition in this action is correct, with the following exceptions: *(Give particulars. If no exceptions, state "None.")*

   None

3. I am aware that I am not obliged to give evidence that I have committed adultery. I am willing to give that evidence.

SWORN BEFORE ME AT   )
The City of Toronto   )

in the Municipality of   )
Metropolitan Toronto   )

this _2nd_ day of _May_ 19_9-_   ) _John Que Public_

J M Commissioner   ~~Petitioner's signature~~

A Commissioner for taking Affidavits, etc.   Respondent's signature

Court file no. _____

ONTARIO COURT (GENERAL DIVISION)

BETWEEN:

Joan Public

PETITIONER
(Wife   )

-and-

John Que Public

RESPONDENT
(Husband   )

REQUISITION

To the Registrar at the __Municipality of Metropolitan Toronto__

- I request you to issue a Certificate of Divorce in the above title of proceeding commenced at __Toronto__ ;
- Affidavit attached;
- Copy of Divorce Judgment, as issued, attached/

THIS SECTION FOR OFFICE USE ONLY

I HAVE SEARCHED THE COURT RECORDS PURSUANT TO RULE 70.22 (c) AND HAVE ASCERTAINED THAT THERE IS NO INDICATION THAT THE AFFIDAVIT FILED IS INCORRECT

This _____ day _____ 19 ____

Local Registrar

Per: _____
Senior Counter Clerk

Date:

Firm Name:

Address:

Tel. No:

SCP-DIVONT-SOLE(15-1)97

Court file no. _____

ONTARIO COURT (GENERAL DIVISION)

BETWEEN:

Joan Public

PETITIONER

(Wife)

-and-

RESPONDENT

John Que Public

(Husband)

AFFIDAVIT

I, Joan Public , of the City of Toronto

in the Municipality of Toronto

MAKE OATH AND SAY (or AFFIRM):

1. I am the Petitioner herein and as such have knowledge of the matters hereinafter deposed to.
2. No appeal from the divorce is pending.
3. No order has been made extending the time for appealing from the divorce.

SWORN BEFORE ME at the _____)
)
of _____ in the)
)
_____) _____
)
this ____ day of _____19 _____)

_____
A Commissioner for taking Affidavits, etc.

SCP-DIVONT-SOLE(16-1)97

110

Court file no._____

ONTARIO COURT (GENERAL DIVISION)

BETWEEN:

Joan Public   **PETITIONER**
(Wife   )

- and -

(Court seal)

John Que Public   **RESPONDENT**
(Husband   )

UNDERTAKING NOT TO APPEAL

We, the undersigned, do hereby agree, in the event that the Divorce Judgment is granted by this Honourable Court, to the granting of a Divorce Judgment forthwith and do hereby undertake that no appeal will be taken from the said Divorce Judgment. We understand that if the Divorce Judgment is made final at trial neither of us will thereafter be able to make application for a division of the family assets under the Family Law Act and that we will be forever barred from doing so.

Dated at Toronto, this ___3rd___ day of ___July, 199-___

WITNESS:

_J C Ewe_____   _Joan Public_____

_JM Witness_____   _John Que Public_____

judge who will be handling your case. From this, you will see what information the judge wants and in what order he or she wants it. Take notes and modify the general explanation set out below to suit your own circumstances.

When you appear before the judge, take your reference notes so that you don't forget anything. If you want to use this book as an aid, it is probably wiser to tear out the applicable pages rather than take the whole book in with you. Judges seem to have an aversion to watching people read their case out of a book or from a printed sheet of instructions. The best procedure is to use notes; but use them just to remind you what the next point is and then state the point in your own language.

A better technique is to point out to a judge at the start of the trial that you are representing yourself and request that he or she lead you through the proceedings. Fortunately, your chances of getting co-operation are good if you have prepared your documents correctly.

Because lawyers are called in order of seniority, your case will be put at the bottom of the list and will usually be the last of the day. Therefore, there will be only the judge, you, the clerk, and whatever witnesses you have in the court. This makes it a more informal hearing.

1. Your testimony

Always address the judge as "Your Honour" before a judge of the Ontario Court (General Division). If the judge is a woman, ask the court beforehand how she is to be addressed: usually she will be referred to as "Your Honour."

When the judge calls your case, you will step up to the front of the courtroom, introduce yourself, and state that you are acting on your own behalf. In most cases, the judge will lead you through the proceedings. You will be asked to take the stand and give the court the following information orally.

Reconciliation

Is there any possibility of reconciliation? If your answer is no, you may also be asked, "Why not?"

Particulars of marriage

Be prepared to relate the particulars of the marriage. For example —

(a) I was married at Toronto, Ontario, on July 29, 1977.

(b) My surname before marriage was Public; or my wife's surname before marriage was Smith.

(c) My surname at birth was Smith.

(d) At the time of the marriage I had never been married before.

(e) At the time of the marriage my husband/wife had never been married before. (Reference will also be made to your marriage registration certificate. Simply state that it is a true copy of the registration of the marriage and that the facts given on it are correct.)

Residence

(a) I reside at (give your address).

(b) I have resided in Ontario since (give date) and I regard the province as my permanent home.

(c) During the 12 months before starting this action, I lived at (give address).

Grounds for divorce

(a) I am seeking divorce from my (husband/wife) on the grounds of marriage breakdown based on (give here the section as set out in your Petition).

(b) My (wife/husband) and I separated on (give date).

(c) I have not lived with my (wife/husband) since that time; or I lived with my (wife/husband) for two months after the separation in an effort to reconcile.

(d) The particulars of my grounds for divorce are (give details of your allegations of adultery or cruelty).

Children

If there are children of the marriage, identify them by giving their full names and dates of birth. If there are no children of the marriage, clearly state this.

Tell the court who has custody of the children, who they are being supported by, what schools they attend, and what you propose regarding future custody and upbringing. If you are asking for custody, you should mention whether or not you wish your spouse to have visiting rights. If your spouse has custody of the children, you should say whether or not you wish access to the children.

Other proceedings

If there have been no other petitions or proceedings with reference to the marriage, simply say so. If there have been other proceedings, simply state the nature of these proceedings, and the outcome.

Separation agreements and financial arrangements

If there are no such agreements, say so. If you have an informal (oral) agreement for the respondent to pay support to you, state the amount received each month. If you have a formal separation agreement, have your copy of the agreement with you and hand it to the judge.

Collusion, connivance, and condonation

Be sure you know the meaning of these words before you go into court! (See the Glossary at the end of this book.) Make the following statements.

(a) There is no collusion or connivance between my (wife/husband) and me with regard to these proceedings.

(b) I have not forgiven my (wife/husband) for the adultery and/or cruelty.

(c) I have not stood idly by and encouraged the adultery or cruelty.

In conclusion, simply tell the court that you want a Divorce Judgment and any of the following that are applicable:

(a) Custody of the children

(b) Support

(c) Costs

(d) Anything else applicable to your case

2. Your witnesses' testimony

In most cases, witnesses are required to corroborate testimony. If you have a witness, you should have him or her called to the witness box and sworn in by the clerk after you have completed your own testimony. Then do the following:

(a) Ask the witness whether he or she knows your spouse.

(b) Ask your witness to tell the court of his or her personal knowledge of the allegation of cruelty or adultery, or the period of separation contained in your Petition.

You should always know what your witness is going to say. Interview him or her before the court appearance to ensure that there will be no surprises in the testimony.

In most cases, your witnesses will be either personal friends or acquaintances who will not present too great a problem. If your case is going to be based on the testimony of a hostile or unfriendly witness, you must retain a lawyer to conduct the court hearing. In addition, the witness should be subpoenaed to ensure his or her presence at the trial. If everything goes all right at your trial, the judge should grant your Divorce Judgment along with any other orders such as custody and support. Take careful note of what the judge says because it is up to you (or your lawyer if you decide to hire one for the trial only) to prepare the Divorce Judgment. If you are representing yourself and you miss what the judge says (which is very easy to do), ask if you can see your Trial Record following the trial. The judge will have written down the order on the back of the Record. This may be obtained from the clerk immediately following the trial or from the registrar of the court.

If the judge reserves judgment, it may mean that he or she is not satisfied about some point and wants to consider it further or that he or she is giving you a chance to correct a defect and appear at a later date. Usually, the judge will also instruct you to see a lawyer. If so, you will have no alternative but to do so.

You then proceed to draft the Divorce Judgment according to what the judge has ordered, present it to the court clerk who will check it against the Record to make sure that it is exactly in accordance with the judge's order. The court clerk will send it out to all parties. (Remember, you must provide stamped, addressed envelopes.)

The Certificate of Divorce can be obtained 31 days after the date of the Divorce Judgment.

h. WHAT NAME CAN A WIFE USE?

When a woman marries, she is entitled to continue to use her maiden name or, at her option, may legally use her husband's name. Even if she adopts her husband's name, she cannot legally be prevented from reverting to her maiden name at any time. These rights evolve from the principle that a person may use whatever name he or she chooses, as long as it is not for fraudulent purposes.

Practically, however, it is usually difficult for a wife to convince appropriate authorities (e.g., passport office, motor vehicle licence bureau) to change her official documents to her maiden name without either a court order or a Divorce Judgment. Once you have obtained your Divorce Judgment, simply show this document to the appropriate authorities.

6

THE ONTARIO COURT (GENERAL DIVISION) FAMILY COURT

If you and/or your spouse live in Hamilton, London, Barrie, Kingston, and/or Napanee, you are in an area under the jurisdiction of the Ontario Court (General Division) Family Court ("Family Court"), formerly the Unified Family Court. The forms required to process an uncontested divorce in Family Court are different, some say simpler, than those required in all other jurisdictions. There is no joint petition in Family Court.

The forms required for Family Court are the following:

(a) Application (see Sample #32)

(b) Financial Statement (see Sample #33)

(c) Notice of Hearing (Divorce) (see Sample #34)

(d) Acknowledgment of Service (see Sample #35)

(e) Affidavit of Service (see Sample #36)

(f) Affidavit of Applicant (see Sample #37)

(g) Application Record (see Sample #38)

(h) Divorce Judgment (see Sample #39)

(i) Affidavit for Certificate of Divorce (see Sample #40)

(j) Certificate of Divorce (see Sample #41)

(k) Support Deduction Order (see Sample #13)

(l) Support Deduction Order Information Form (see Sample #14)

(**Note:** The Support Deduction Order and the Support Deduction Order Information

Form are the same for both the Ontario Court (General Division) Family Court and the Ontario Court (General Division).

If you live in one of these cities, you can still file for divorce in the Ontario Court (General Division) in a different judicial district unless there are children involved. If children are involved, the papers must be filed in the area where the children live. As well, if a trial is necessary, it must be held in the jurisdiction where you or your spouse live. In summary, if you live in Hamilton, London, Barrie, Kingston, or Napanee and wish to file for divorce, you are likely to be required to complete the forms set out here.

Although the forms differ, the concepts of obtaining an uncontested divorce in the Family Court are similar to those in other jurisdictions. I therefore recommend that you follow the outline provided here, substituting the Family Court forms for the Ontario Court (General Division) forms where applicable. In reading the material about the Ontario Court (General Division), please note that the person beginning the proceedings is referred to as the "Petitioner," whereas in the Family Court, that person is referred to as the "Applicant."

The courts also differ slightly in their procedures, such as how they wish the Application Record to be set up. At the time you issue your originating documents, you may wish to check with the court clerk in your own jurisdiction to confirm the particular procedures and to make sure there have not been any changes. This is a new court, and is it still in its initial stages, so it is conceivable that changes will occur to its procedures.

If you are filing in Family Court, you will still need to read the rest of this book so that you have an understanding of the process. However, keep the following in mind. First, the Application replaces the Petition for Divorce. As you read the Application (see Sample #32), you will notice that you are required to complete and file a Financial Statement like the one shown in Sample #33 and file it with the Application if you are claiming child or spousal support, or have any other monetary claims.

You should take the Notice of Hearing (Divorce) (Sample #34) with you to court (with the information pertaining to the applicant and respondent filled out at the top of the document) when you go to issue the Application. You should also take a copy of your Financial Statement with you, if monetary claims are being made. The court registrar will provide you with the date of hearing and complete the Notice of Hearing at that time.

The cost to issue the Application is $135*, which is payable to the Minister of Finance by cash, money order, or certified cheque. At this point, if you have your original marriage certificate, you should file it with the court.

The Notice of Hearing, together with the Application and Financial Statement (if applicable), must then be served on the respondent after the documents are issued. The manner of serving the documents is set out in section **d.6.** of chapter 5.

Once the documents are served, the recipient of the documents may either acknowledge service by completing and signing the Acknowledgment of Service (Sample #35), or the process server may

complete an Affidavit of Service (Sample #36).

If your spouse has not filed any responding documents by the prescribed amount of time shown on the Application (i.e., 20 days if served in Ontario, 40 days if served in another province or state, and 60 days if served elsewhere in the world), you can proceed for an uncontested divorce.

The date of the hearing provided by the court should have been far enough in advance that it will not have expired by the time you get to this step. If the date is approaching and you are not yet ready to proceed, you can simply fax a letter to the court requesting that it extend the date of the hearing; provide a reason why it should do so. This way, you avoid an unnecessary court appearance.

Before the return court date, if your spouse has not contested the Application, you can set the matter down for hearing. You will need to pay the court $255*. Again, a certified cheque or money order must be made payable to the Minister of Finance. The court will also accept cash.

You must file with the court the original Application, Financial Statement (if applicable), and Affidavit of the Applicant (Sample #37, unless you wish to attend in person), along with a copy of a draft Divorce Judgment (Sample #39), stapled together with a front page entitled "Application Record" (see Sample #38), which lists an index of the documents contained in the Record. Some courts, the Hamilton court for example, also require a blank sheet of paper with the word "Endorsement" typed at the top.

At this point, you also file the Affidavit of Service of the documents that were served on the Respondent, and the original marriage certificate if you did not file it when you issued the Application.

---

* Note that all fees are subject to change without notice. Please check all fees with the court or appropriate government office before submitting funds.

You will also file (separate from the Record) four copies of the Divorce Judgment, and if a claim for support is being made, one copy each of a Support Deduction Order (see Sample #15) and a Support Deduction Order Information Form (see Sample #16). You also need to supply two stamped self-addressed envelopes, one envelope addressed to you, one addressed to your spouse.

You do not need to appear in court if you set out your evidence in an Affidavit of Applicant and file it with the court as part of the Application Record. You can, however, appear before a judge to give your evidence in person on the trial date set by the court.

The sample of the Divorce Judgment shown (Sample #39) is for a divorce only. If additional claims have been made, further clauses must also be added. See the sample of the Divorce Judgment in the General Division (Sample #24) for clauses for support and custody.

Once you receive the issued Divorce Judgment in the mail from the court, apply for a Certificate of Divorce 31 days after the date of Judgment. To do this, take a copy of your Divorce Judgment, the Affidavit for Certificate of Divorce (see Sample #40), and a completed Certificate of Divorce (see Sample #41) to the court, along with a further $17*. The court will then issue the Certificate.

---

* Note that all fees are subject to change without notice. Please check all fees with the court or appropriate government office before submitting funds.

SAMPLE #32
APPLICATION FOR FAMILY COURT

Ontario Court (General Division)
Family Court

Application

Family Court Rules **Form 8   Page 1**

Court file number

Applicant(s) *If more than one applicant, give name and address for each.*

Full name Joan Public	Full name
Address for service *(street, number, municipality, postal code)* **322 Lakeshore Road** **London, Ontario L5N 3N2**	Address for service *(street, number, municipality, postal code)*
Lawyer *(name, address and phone no.)*	*< put telephone number here >*

Respondent(s) *If more than one respondent, give name and address for each and for lawyer if known.*

Full name John Que Public	Full name
Address for service *(street, number, municipality, postal code)* **1000 Yonge Street** **London, Ontario L5N 3N1**	Address for service *(street, number, municipality, postal code)*
Lawyer *(name, address and phone no.)*	Lawyer *(name, address and phone no.)*

---

1. I ask for:

1a [X] a divorce from the respondent

Full name
John Que Public

We were married on *(date)*
December 27, 1984

at *(place)*
London, Ontario

We last lived together on *(date)*
June 1, 1995

Our marriage certificate
[X] has been filed with the Court
[ ] has not been filed with the Court, but will be filed before the hearing.
[ ] cannot be filed with the Court. It is impossible to obtain a certificate because: *(Give reason)*

1b [X] support under the *Divorce Act*
1b i [ ] for me
1b ii [X] for the following child(ren)

Full name(s)	Birthdate(s)
Robert John Public	June 1, 1985

1c [X] custody
1c i [X] of the child(ren) listed in 1b
1c ii [ ] of the following child(ren)

Full name(s)	Birthdate(s)
Robert John Public	June 1, 1985

1d [ ] visiting rights (access) to the following child(ren)

Full name(s)	Birthdate(s)

1e [X] support under the *Family Law Act*
1e i [ ] for me
1e ii [X] for the following child(ren)

Full name(s)	Birthdate(s)
Robert John Public	June 1, 1985

1f [X] custody under *Children's Law Reform Act*
1f i [X] of the child(ren) listed in 1e
1f ii [ ] of the following child(ren)

Full name(s)	Birthdate(s)
Robert John Public	June 1, 1985

1g [ ] visiting rights (access) under *Children's Law Reform Act* to the following child(ren)

Full name(s)	Birthdate(s)

FC 0008 (page 1 of 3) DIVORCEmate Software Inc.

Ontario Court (General Division)
Family Court

Application

Family Court Rules **Form 8** Page 2

Court file number

1h		a division of property	1k		annulment of my marriage to the respondent which took place on *(date)*	1m		restraining my spouse/former spouse from harassing or communicating with me or children in my lawful custody.
1i		exclusive possession of the matrimonial home at *(address)*			at *(place)*	1n		restraining my spouse from depleting his/her property.
1j		exclusive possession of contents of the matrimonial home at (address)	1l		indexing of an existing support order	1o		court costs, including costs paid on my behalf by third parties, to whom I assign such costs collected.
				X	indexing of the support sought in 1e			

1p		other *(specify)*

2.

		Applicant	Respondent Spouse
2a	If married, surname immediately before marriage	n\a	n\a
2b	Surname at birth	Jones	Public
2c	Marital status at time of our marriage *(if divorced, give place and date of divorce)*	never married	never married
2d	Birthplace	Windsor, Ontario	Windsor, Ontario
2e	Birthdate	April 11, 1965	May 12, 1954
2f	Place of actual residence *(Municipality and province)*	County of Middlesex, Ontario	County of Middlesex, Ontario
2g	Period of habitual residence in Ontario immediately before filing Application	since birth	since birth

3. The following are all living children of the marriage as defined by the *Divorce Act* or children of the parties, if unmarried.

Full name(s)	Birthdate(s)
Robert John Public	June 1, 1986

Place of ordinary residence of the children *(Municipality and province)*
County of Middlesex, Ontario

4. The following information relates to the children:

Name of child	School and grade/year	Person with whom child lives	Length of time child has lived there
Robert John Public	The Great School Grade 4	Child resides with the Applicant	Child has resided with Applicant since separation,

5. The person(s) for whose benefit this Application is made is/are:

Full name(s)	Relationship to applicant	Relationship to respondent
Robert John Public	son	son

Ontario Court (General Division)
Family Court

_____

Application
Family Court Rules **Form 8** Page 3

Court file number
_____

6. There has never been any court action for divorce, annulment, alimony, maintenance, support, custody, access, division of property, possession of the matrimonial home or contents, a restraining order or other matrimonial matter between the respondent and me, or between the respondent and any person for whose benefit a claim is made in this Application, except: _(Give date, name of court, court file number, nature of case. If no other proceedings, state "None".)_
None
_____
_____
_____
_____
_____

7. The respondent and I have entered into the following written or oral agreement or understanding in respect of the claims made in this Application _(Give details. If no agreement or understanding, state "None".)_
None
_____
_____
_____
_____
_____

8. The grounds for this Application are as follows: _(Give details of grounds. Attach an additional page if necessary.)_
Custody: The child of the marriage resides with the wife and has resided with her since the parties separated. The husband has liberal and generous access to the child, and exercises access every second weekend from Friday night until Sunday night. The wife is in a better position to meet the child's day–to–day needs, and has been the child's primary caretaker since birth. The child is happy and well adjusted in the present circumstances, is doing well in school, and it would be in his best interests that the present situation does not change.

Child Support: The husband earns $50,000.00 per year. In accordance with the Child Support Guidelines he is required to pay $414.00 per month support, not taxable to either party.
_____
_____
_____
_____
_____
_____

_____   _____
Date   _Signature_

_____   _____
Date   _Signature_

Where the applicant claims support, custody of a child or a division of property, this form must be accompanied by a Financial Statement in Form 9.

Ontario Court (General Division) Family Court

Financial Statement

Family Court Rules   Form 9   Page 1

Court file no.

Address _____

I, _____ , of _____
   Name   *(address — street & number, municipality, postal code)*

_____

declare that details of my financial situation and all my property are accurately set out below, to the best of my knowledge and belief.

Monthly Income	Actual	Proposed	Monthly Expenses	Actual	Proposed		Actual	Proposed
Gross Pay *before Deductions*	$	$	**Food** Groceries and household supplies	$	$	**Transportation** Public transit, taxis, etc. $	$	
Family Allowance	$	$	Meals outside the home	$	$	Car operation Gas and oil $	$	
Tenants or Boarders	$	$	**Clothing**	$	$	Insurance and licence $	$	
Pension	$	$	**Laundry and Dry cleaning**	$	$	Mainten-ance $	$	
Workmen's Compensation	$	$	**Housing** Rent or Mortgage	$	$	**Life Insurance** $	$	
Public Assistance	$	$	Taxes	$	$	**Education & Recreation** School fees, books, etc. $	$	
Investments	$	$	Home Insurance	$	$	Music lessons, hockey, etc. $	$	
Other	$	$	Fuel (heat)	$	$	Newspapers, publications, stationery $	$	
Total Income from all sources A	$	$	Water	$	$	Entertainment, recreation $	$	
Less Deductions Income Tax	$	$	Hydro	$	$	Alcohol, tobacco $	$	
Union Dues	$	$	Phone	$	$	Vacation $	$	
Unemployment Insurance	$	$	Cable T.V.	$	$	**Personal care** Hairdresser, barber $	$	
O.H.I.P.	$	$	Repairs and mainten-ance	$	$	Toilet articles (hairspray, soap, etc.) $	$	
Pension Plans	$	$	Other	$	$	**Babysitting, Day care** $	$	
Canada Pension	$	$	**Health & Medical** Insurance, O.H.I.P.	$	$	Children's allowances, Gifts $	$	
Credit Union Loan	$	$	Drugs	$	$	Support payments to other relatives $	$	
Savings Plans	$	$	Dental care	$	$	Savings for the future (excluding payroll deductions) $	$	
Other	$	$	**Debts** see p. 3	$	$	Miscellaneous $	$	
Total Deductions B	$	$		$	$	**Total** $	$	
Net (Take Home) Income A—B	$	$		$	$			
				$	$			
				$	$			
				$	$			

Name and address of employer

_____

Ontario Court (General Division)
Family Court

Financial Statement

Family Court Rules   **Form 9**   **Page 2**

Court file no.

_____

Address

Details of property
(Show gross values here and show mortgages and other encumbrances under Debts and other liabilities on page 3.)

Land *(including rented premises)*

Address of property   Kind of property   Estimated Value

Date of Marriage   Valuation Date   Date of Statement

Household furniture, appliances, jewellery and automobiles

Description   Estimated Value

Date of Marriage   Valuation Date   Date of Statement

Savings, pensions, R.R.S.P.'s, other savings plans and cash

Item   Institution   Account Number   Maturity   Estimated Value

Date of Marriage   Valuation Date   Date of Statement

Stocks, bonds and other securities

Number   Description   Estimated Value

Date of Marriage   Valuation Date   Date of Statement

Insurance

Kind   Company   Policy Number   Face Amount   Estimated Value

Date of Marriage   Valuation Date   Date of Statement

Ontario Court (General Division)
Family Court

Financial Statement

Family Court Rules   **Form 9**   **Page 3**

Court file no.

_____
Address

Business interests

Name of firm or company	Interest	Estimated Value		
		Date of Marriage	Valuation Date	Date of Statement

Accounts receivable

Particulars	Amount		
	Date of Marriage	Valuation Date	Date of Statement

Other

Kind of Property	Particulars	Estimated Value		
		Date of Marriage	Valuation Date	Date of Statement

Debts and other liabilities

Category	Particulars	Amount		
		Date of Marriage	Valuation Date	Date of Statement

123

Ontario Court (General Division)
Family Court

Financial Statement

Family Court Rules   **Form 9**   **Page 4**

Court file no.

_____

Address

Net value of my property owned on date of marriage

Category	Particulars	Net Value on Date of Marriage

Excluded property

Category	Particulars	Estimated Value on Valuation Day

Disposal of property *(Disposal during the two years preceding this statement or during the marriage, whichever period is shorter)*

Category	Particulars	Estimated Value

And I make this solemn declaration conscientiously believing it to be true and knowing it is of the same force and effect as if made under oath.

Declared before me at the _____ of _____

in the _____ of _____

this _____ day of _____ 19 ___. _____

A Commissioner, etc.

_____
Signature
(This form is to be signed before a lawyer, justice of the peace, notary public or commissioner for taking affidavits.)

NOTICE OF HEARING (DIVORCE) FOR FAMILY COURT

Ontario Court (General Division)
Family Court

80 Dundas Street, London, Ontario

Notice of Hearing (Divorce)
Family Court Rules **Form 30**

Court file number

Applicant(s) *If more than one applicant, give name and address for each.*

Full name Joan Public	Full name
Address for service *(street, number, municipality, postal code)* 322 Lakeshore Road London, Ontario L5N 3N2	Address for service *(street, number, municipality, postal code)*
Lawyer *(name, address and phone no.)*	

Respondent(s) *If more than one respondent, give name and address for each and for lawyer if known.*

Full name John Que Public	Full name
Address for service *(street, number, municipality, postal code)* 1000 Yonge Street London, Ontario L5N 3N1	Address for service *(street, number, municipality, postal code)*

To the Respondent(s)

An Application for a divorce has been filed against you in this court. The details are set out in the attached copy.

The court will hold a hearing

at _____
Address

on _____
Date

at _____ or as soon thereafter as the matter can be heard.
Time

If you dispute the claims made in the Application, you must serve an Answer on the applicant(s) and file it, with proof of service in the court office.

(a)   where this Notice was served on you in Ontario, **within 20 days** after it was served;

(b)   where this Notice was served on you in Canada outside Ontario or in the United States of America, **within 40 days** after it was served; or

(c)   where this Notice was served on you outside Canada and the United States of America, **within 60 days** after it was served.

If a Financial Statement (Form 9) is attached to this Notice, you must file the same form with the court along with your Answer.
If you fail to file an Answer, you may lose your right to support and the court may set a new hearing date without notice to you.
If you fail to appear at the hearing, a divorce may be granted in your absence and an order may be made and enforced against you.
Neither spouse is free to remarry until the court has granted a divorce.

_____
Date

_____
Clerk of the Court

SAMPLE #35
ACKNOWLEDGMENT OF SERVICE FOR FAMILY COURT

Ontario Court (General Division)
Family Court

80 Dundas Street, London, Otnario

Acknowledgment of Service
Family Court Rules **Form 1**

Court file number

I, __John Que Public__ am a person named as
Name

[ ] an applicant
in the documents indicated below.
[X] a respondent

My address for service of further documents is: *(street and number, municipality, postal code)*

_____

_____

_____

_____

I have received a copy today of the documents checked and indicated below by my initials.

[X] Application

[X] Notice of Hearing

[X] Financial Statement

[ ] Financial Statement in Blank Form

[ ] Net Family Property Statement

[ ] Net Family Property Statement in Blank Form

[ ] Answer

[ ] Answer in Blank Form

[ ] Notice to Added Party

[ ] Reply by Added Party

[ ] Reply by Applicant

[ ] Order on Motion Without Notice

[ ] Affidavit in Support of Motion

[ ] Notice of Motion

[ ] Certificate of Pending Litigation

[ ] Summons to a Witness

[ ] Children's Lawyer's Report

[ ] Other *(Specify)*

_____

_____

_____

_____

_____   _____
Signature of person acknowledging service   *Date*

You are requested to complete and sign this form and mail it immediately to the court address shown above.

AFFIDAVIT OF SERVICE FOR FAMILY COURT

Ontario Court (General Division)	Affidavit of Service
Family Court	*Family Court Rules* **Form 12**

80 Dundas Street, London, Ontario _____

Court file number _____

Applicant(s)
JOAN PUBLIC   **WIFE**

Respondent(s)
JOHN QUE PUBLIC   **HUSBAND**

I, __John Smith__ of the __City__ of __London__
    Full name   *City, town, etc*   *Name*

in the __County__ of __Middlesex__, make oath and say:
   County, regional municipality, etc.   *Name*

On *(date)*
July 1, 1997
I served *(name of person served)*
John Que Public

with the following document(s): *(specify)*
Notice of Hearing
Application
Financial Statement
[X] by leaving a copy with him/her at
(address)
1000 Yonge Street, London, Ontario

In response to my request to produce identification, the person served *(state what identification produced or give other response of person served.)*
confirmed that he was the Respondent
in these proceedings.

In response to my request to complete and sign an Acknowledgement of Service, the person served
[ ] complied with my request
[ ] refused to comply with my request
[ ] other *(specify)*

[ ] by leaving a copy with *(name)*

a person apparently of the age of 16 years or over, at *(address)*

and by mailing a copy on *(date)*

to the person to be served at the same address. I previously made unsuccessful attempts at personal service on *(date)*

at *(address)*

and on *(date)*

at *(address)*

[ ] by leaving a copy with *(name)*

a person apparently of the age of 16 years or over, at *(address)*

[ ] by mailing a copy to him/her at *(address)*

the address for service shown on the document dated *(date)*

filed by him/her in the proceeding bearing court file no.

[ ] by telephone transmission to *(name)*

at *(telephone no.)*

[ ] by leaving a copy at *(address)*

the address for service shown on the document dated *(date)*

filed by him/her in the proceeding bearing court file no.

[ ] by mailing a copy to *(solicitor's name)*

the solicitor acting for him/her, at *(address)*

[ ] by leaving a copy with *(name)*

the *(position or title)*

of that corporation, at *(address)*

To effect service it was necessary for me to travel
_____ **kilometres**

Sworn before me at the
City of __London__

in the **County** of __Middlesex__

on __July 2__ 19__97__

_____
A Commissioner, etc.

_____
Signature
(this form must be signed before a lawyer, notary public or commissioner for taking affidavits.)

Ontario Court (General Division)   Affidavit of Applicant
Family Court
                                                    Court file number
80 Dundas Street, London, Ontario

Applicant

Joan Public
322 Lakeshore Road
London, Ontario
L5N 3N2

Respondent

John Que Public
1000 Yonge Street
London, Ontario
L5N 3N1

AFFIDAVIT OF APPLICANT

I, **Joan Public** of the City of London of County of Middlesex, Province of Ontario, MAKE OATH AND SAY:

1.   There is no possibility of the reconciliation of myself and my spouse because we have irreconcilable differences and our marriage has broken down, as evidenced by the fact that we have lived separate and apart since on or about June 1, 1995 and continue to live separate and apart. I do not want to reconcile.

2.   All the information in the Application in this action is correct with the following exceptions: **none**

3.   The certificate of marriage filed in this action was issued on December 27, 1984 bearing license number C53219. The said certificate of marriage correctly contains the particular of our marriage.

4.   The grounds for the divorce are as follows: Separation for a period of no less than one year.

2

5.   There has been no agreement, conspiracy, understanding or arrangement to which I am either directly or indirectly a party for the purpose of subverting the administration of justice, fabricating or suppressing evidence or deceiving the court.

6.   That I do not wish to claim a division of property at this time and I am aware that a claim for division of property may be barred after the divorce.

7.   The following are the present and proposed custody and access arrangements:

The child of the marriage, Robert John Public, born June 1, 1986, has resided with me since separation. The Respondent has access to our son every second weekend from Friday evening until Sunday evening, as well as at other times that are mutually agreeable upon between us. I propose that I have custody of Robert John Public and that the Respondent have liberal and generous access to the child.

8.   The following are the present and proposed support arrangements for myself and the children of the marriage:

The Respondent has been paying me $400.00 per month for the support of our child since our separation. I propose that the Respondent continue to pay support in this amount.

9.   The last known address of the Respondent is as follows:

1000 Yonge Street, London, Ontario L5N 3N1.

I known this to be the address because: This is the address where the Respondent was served with the herein Application, and is the address where he exercises access to our son.

SWORN before me at the City	)
of London	)
in the County	)
of Middlesex	)
this 15th day of January, 1997	) **JOAN PUBLIC**

_____
A Commissioner for taking Affidavits, etc.

Ontario Court (General Division)   Application Record
Family Court   *Family Court Rules*
                                                                    Court file number

80 Dundas Street, London, Ontario

Applicant

Joan Public
322 Lakeshore Road
London, Ontario L5N 3N2

Respondent

John Que Public
1000 Yonge Street
London, Ontario
L5N 3N1

APPLICATION RECORD

INDEX

1.   Application

2.   Financial Statement of Applicant sworn June 16, 1996

3.   Affidavit of Applicant sworn August 16, 1996

4.   Draft Divorce Judgment

DIVORCE JUDGMENT (Family Court)

Ontario Court (General Division)	**Divorce Judgment**
Family Court	*Family Court Rules* **Form 34**

80 Dundas Street, London, Ontario

Judge	

Applicant(s) *If more than one applicant, give name and address for each.*

Full name	Full name
Joan Public	
Address for service *(street, number, municipality, postal code)* 322 Lakeshore Road London, Ontario L5N 3N2	Address for service *(street, number, municipality, postal code)*
Lawyer *(name, address and phone no.)*	

Date of Judgment

Court file number

Respondent(s) *If more than one respondent, give name and address for each and for lawyer if known.*

Full name	Full name
John Que Public	
Address for service *(street, number, municipality, postal code)* 1000 Yonge Street London, Ontario L5N 3N1	Address for service *(street, number, municipality, postal code)*
Lawyer *(name, address and phone no.)*	Lawyer *(name, address and phone no.)*

On the application of *(name)*   **Joan Public**

heard on *(date)*

and on considering the evidence and the submissions on behalf of *(names)*

Joan Public, no one appearing on behalf of the Respondent,

This court orders that *(name)*   **JOAN PUBLIC**

and *(name)*   **JOHN QUE PUBLIC**

who were married at *(place)*   **London, Ontario**

on *(date)*   **December 27, 1984**

be divorced and that the divorce take effect   31   days after the date of this order.

Date of signature   Signature of Judge

Neither spouse is free to remarry until this Judgment takes effect, at which time you may obtain a Certificate of Divorce from the court office.

FC 0034 DIVORCEmate Software Inc.

Ontario Court (General Division)
Family Court

Affidavit for Certificate of Divorce
Family Court Rules
Court file number

80 Dundas Street, London, Ontario

Applicant

Joan Public
322 Lakeshore Road
London, Ontario L5N 3N2

Respondent

John Que Public
1000 Yonge Street
London, Ontario
L5N 3N1

A F F I D A V I T

I, **JOAN PUBLIC**, of the City of London, in the County of Middlesex, **MAKE OATH**

AND SAY:

1.   I am the Applicant herein and as such have knowledge of the matters hereinafter

deposed to.

2.   No appeal from the divorce is pending.

3.   No order has been made extending the time for appealing from the divorce.

SWORN BEFORE ME at the City   )
of London, in the   )
County of Middlesex   )   _____
this   day of   199-   )   **Joan Public**

A Commissioner etc.

Ontario Court (General Division)
Family Court

80 Dundas Street, London, Ontario _____

Certificate of Divorce
Family Court Rules Form 35

Court file number
_____

CERTIFICATE OF DIVORCE

This is to certify that the marriage of   JOAN PUBLIC _____

and JOHN QUE PUBLIC _____

which was solemnized at   LONDON, ONTARIO _____

on DECEMBER 27, 1984 _____, was dissolved by an order of this court

which became effective on   _____

_____   _____
Date   Signature (Clerk of the Court)

FC 0035 DIVORCEmate Software Inc.

APPENDIX 1
STEP-BY-STEP CHECKLIST
FOR A TYPICAL DIVORCE

☐ Read the *Divorce Guide* carefully to determine whether or not your case is suitable for you to represent yourself.

☐ Purchase a package of forms at your book or department store or from the publisher (see order form at the front of the book), or if you are filing in Family Court, contact the courthouse for the forms. **Note:** There are two different packages available: one for sole petitioners, and one for joint petitioners. If you and/or your spouse live in Hamilton, London, Barrie, Kingston, and/or Napanee, you must contact the courthouse for the correct forms. Please note that there is no joint petition in Family Court; if you are filing in Family Court jurisdiction, you must file as a sole petitioner (applicant).

☐ Read through this book to determine which procedure you are going to follow and be sure to purchase the correct kit.

☐ Write for a copy of your Certificate of Marriage. If you live in Toronto, Sault Ste. Marie, or Windsor, prepare the Case Information Statement.

☐ If the marriage for which you are seeking a divorce was outside Ontario, obtain a copy of a previous Certificate of Divorce for either party previously married.

IF YOU ARE PROCEEDING AS JOINT PETITIONERS IN ONTARIO COURT (GENERAL DIVISION)

☐ Complete and check rough draft of Petition using information from Certificate of Marriage. Make a good copy and photocopy two copies.

☐ Prepare Record. Prepare Support Deduction Order and the Support Deduction Order Information Form. If you live in Toronto, Sault Ste. Marie, or Windsor, prepare the Case Information Statement.

☐ File Petition, Record, and all other documents, pay fees, and set action down. Be sure to send along with your documents stamped, addressed envelopes for each of the parties (including yourself).

☐ Upon receipt of Divorce Judgment, wait 31 days and file Certificate of Divorce.

IF YOU ARE PROCEEDING AS SOLE PETITIONER IN ONTARIO COURT (GENERAL DIVISION)

☐ Confirm your spouse's address and all the information needed for your Petition. Find address of other person if needed.

☐ Obtain a picture of your spouse if service may prove to be difficult.

☐ Complete and check rough draft of Petition using information from Certificate of Marriage. Make a good copy and one photocopy, then sign both the original and the copy.

☐ Take Certificate of Marriage and Petition to registrar's office and pay fees.

☐ Make necessary number of photocopies of original signed and sealed Petition.

☐ Take necessary number of copies of Petition and photograph to sheriff's office for service on spouse (and other person if necessary) or send to sheriff's office near spouse with covering letter and cheque or money order for $20 to $25.

or

☐ Have Petition served by other means, e.g., process server.

☐ Receive Affidavit of Service with Petition attached from whomever served Petition. Make copy of Affidavit of Service for your records.

☐ Prepare Record. Prepare Support Deduction Order and the Support Deduction Order Information Form.

☐ Wait the length of time required for service, e.g., 20 days or 40 days, and then go to courthouse.

IF YOU ARE PROCEEDING IN ONTARIO COURT (GENERAL DIVISION) FAMILY COURT

☐ Confirm your spouse's address and all the information needed for your application. Find address of other person if needed.

☐ Obtain a picture of your spouse if service may prove to be difficult.

☐ Complete and check rough draft of application using information from Certificate of Marriage. Make a good copy and one photocopy, then sign both the original and the copy.

☐ Complete a Financial Statement if you are claiming child or spousal support, or have any other monetary claims.

- [ ] Take the Notice of Hearing (Divorce), Application, and Financial Statement (if applicable) to court. Get a date of hearing from the court registrar, and complete the Notice of Hearing. Pay fees and file marriage certificate with the court.

- [ ] Serve the Notice of Hearing, Application, and Financial Statement (if applicable) on the respondent.

- [ ] Take necessary number of copies of Application and photograph to sheriff's office for service on spouse (and other person if necessary) or send to sheriff's office near spouse with covering letter and cheque or money order for $20 to $25.

or

- [ ] Have Application served by other means, e.g., process server.

- [ ] Receive Affidavit of Service with Application attached from whomever served Application. Make copy of Affidavit of Service for your records.

- [ ] Prepare Record. Prepare Support Deduction Order and the Support Deduction Order Information Form if applicable. File, along with four copies of Divorce Judgment. Include stamped, self-addressed envelopes.

- [ ] Wait the length of time required for service, e.g., 20 days or 40 days, and then go to courthouse.

Where a court appearance is unnecessary

- [ ] File Record, Affidavit of Service, and all other documents, pay fee, and set action down. Be sure to send along with your documents stamped, addressed envelopes for each of the parties (including yourself).

- [ ] Call registrar's office to find out when the Divorce Judgment will be signed.

- [ ] Upon receipt of Divorce Judgment, wait 31 days and file Certificate of Divorce.

Where a court appearance is necessary

- [ ] File Record, Affidavit of Service, and all other necessary documents, pay fee, and set action down.

- [ ] Call court office to find out when you are scheduled for hearing.

- [ ] Attend uncontested divorce hearings.

☐ One week before your hearing be certain that you have the following:

    (a) Certificate of Marriage

    (b) Original of any separation agreement or court order referred to in the Petition

    (c) A witness
       or
       the agreement of your spouse to appear in court, if you are alleging adultery. (It is a good idea to have a witness for your one-year separation, too.)

☐ If any of the above are missing, call the court office and ask for an adjournment.

☐ The day before your hearing review the sample hearing and your documents. Be sure any needed witnesses will appear.

☐ Go early to court (i.e., no later than 9:30 a.m.) and to the proper courtroom. Note spelling of the presiding judge's name. When your name is called, go up and present your case. Be calm. If all of the other steps are properly done, you should have no problem.

☐ Be sure to note the terms of the Divorce Judgment carefully. See the clerk if necessary.

☐ Type up your Divorce Judgment in accordance with the terms and take it, along with stamped, addressed envelopes for all parties (including yourself and the Children's Lawyer, if one is involved).

☐ Thirty-one days from the date of your Divorce Judgment, you may apply for a Divorce Certificate.

APPENDIX 2
ADDRESSES TO WRITE TO FOR MARRIAGE CERTIFICATES

You will need a certificate as proof of a valid marriage in many of the proceedings described in this book. Here's where to get it.

PROVINCE/TERRITORY	ADDRESS
Alberta	Vital Statistics Division Alberta Municipal Affairs 10365 - 97 Street Edmonton, AB T5J 3W7
British Columbia	Vital Statistics Division Ministry of Health 818 Fort Street Victoria, BC V8W 1H8 (payable to Minister of Finance)
Manitoba	Division of Vital Statistics Consumer and Corporate Affairs 317 - 450 Broadway Winnipeg, MB R3C 0V8
New Brunswick	Registrar General Department of Health and Community Services P.O. Box 5100 Fredericton, NB E3B 5G8
Newfoundland	Vital Statistics Division Department of Health Confederation Building, East Block P.O. Box 8700 St. John's, NF A1B 4J6
Northwest Territories	Registrar General Vital Statistics Department of Safety and Public Services P.O. Box 1320 Yellowknife, NT X1A 2L9
Nova Scotia	Deputy Registrar General Department of Health 1723 Hollis Street P.O. Box 157 Halifax, NS B3J 2M9

Ontario	Registrar General
	Ministry of Consumer and Commercial Relations
	P.O. Box 4600
	Thunder Bay, ON P7B 6L8
	(payable to Minister of Finance)

Ontario

Registrar General
Ministry of Consumer and Commercial Relations
P.O. Box 4600
Thunder Bay, ON   P7B 6L8
(payable to Minister of Finance)

Prince Edward Island

Vital Statistics
Department of Health and Social Services
P.O. Box 2000
Charlottetown, PE   C1A 7N8

Québec

Birth and marriage certificates are issued by the Civil Archives of the judicial district where the event was registered. Contact the address below for a list of the 32 offices in Québec.

Ministère de la Justice
Registre du reference
205, rue Montmagny
Québec, QC   G1N 4T2

Saskatchewan

Division of Vital Statistics
Saskatchewan Health
1919 Rose Street
Regina, SK   S4P 3V7

Yukon

Deputy Registrar General of Vital Statistics
Yukon Health and Social Services
P.O. Box 2703
Whitehorse, YT   Y1A 2C6

APPENDIX 3
COURT ADDRESSES

TORONTO REGION

TORONTO
Court House
393 University Avenue
10th Floor
Toronto
M5G 1E6
(416) 327-5505

CENTRAL EAST REGION

REGIONAL SENIOR JUSTICE
The Hon. Jean L. McFarland
Court House
50 Eagle Street W.
Newmarket
L3Y 6B1
(905) 853-4810

DURHAM
Court House
Whitby
L1N 5S4
(905) 668-6957

HALIBURTON
Attached to Victoria for judicial purposes.

MUSKOKA
Court House
Bracebridge
P1L 1R6
(705) 645-4122

NORTHUMBERLAND
Court House
Cobourg
K9A 4L3
(905) 372-7514

PETERBOROUGH
County Court House
Peterborough
K9H 3M3
(705) 745-0589

SIMCOE
Court House
Barrie
L4M 4T2
(705) 734-2722

VICTORIA
Court House
Lindsay
K9V 4R8
(705) 324-3871

YORK
Court House
Newmarket
L3Y 6B1
(905) 853-4810

CENTRAL SOUTH REGION

REGIONAL SENIOR JUSTICE
The Hon. E. Fedak
Court House
50 Main Street E.
Hamilton
L8N 1E9
(905) 308-7200

BRANT
Court House
Brantford
N3T 2L0
(519) 752-5941

HALDIMAND
Court House
Cayuga
N0A 1E0
(905) 772-5375

HAMILTON-WENTWORTH
Court House
Hamilton
L8N 1E9
(905) 522-9281

NIAGARA NORTH
Court House
St. Catharines
L2R 7N8
(905) 685-4221

NIAGARA SOUTH
Court House
Welland
L3B 3W6
(905) 732-1349

NORFOLK
Court House
Simcoe
N3Y 4L2
(519) 426-6550

WATERLOO
Court House
Kitchener
N2H 1C3
(519) 741-3203

CENTRAL WEST REGION

REGIONAL SENIOR JUSTICE
The Hon. J.D. Carnwath
Court House
7755 Hurontario Street
Brampton
L6V 2M7
(905) 452-6623

BRUCE
Court House
Walkerton
N0G 2V0
(519) 881-0671

DUFFERIN
Court House
Orangeville
L9W 3P9
(519) 941-2991

GREY
Court House
Owen Sound
N4K 3E3
(519) 376-5795

HALTON
Court House
Milton
L9T 1Y7
(905) 878-2813

PEEL
Court House
Brampton
L6V 2M7
(905) 452-6623

WELLINGTON
Court House
Guelph
N1H 3T9
(519) 824-0051

EAST REGION

REGIONAL SENIOR JUSTICE
The Hon. J.B. Chadwick
Court House
161 Elgin Street
Ottawa
K2P 2K1
(613) 239-1400

FRONTENAC
Court House
Kingston
K7L 2N4
(613) 548-6815

HASTINGS
Court House
Belleville
K8N 3A9
(613) 962-8212

LANARK
Court House
Perth
K7H 1G1
(613) 267-1910

LEEDS AND GRENVILLE
Court House
Brockville
K6V 5T7
(613) 342-3535

LENNOX AND ADDINGTON
Court House
Napanee
K7R 1L1
(613) 354-4264

OTTAWA-CARLETON
Court House
Ottawa
K2P 2K1
(613) 239-1400

PRESCOTT AND RUSSELL
Court House
L'Orignal
K0B 1K0
(613) 675-4695

PRINCE EDWARD
Court House
Picton
K0K 2T0
(613) 476-2606

RENFREW
Court House
Pembroke
K8A 6Y6
(613) 735-6886

STORMONT, DUNDAS, AND
GLENGARRY
Court House
Cornwall
K6J 3P2
(613) 933-7500

NORTHEAST REGION

REGIONAL SENIOR JUSTICE
The Hon. Spyros D. Loukidelis
Court House
155 Elm Street West
Sudbury
P3C 1V1
(705) 671-5968

ALGOMA
Court House
Sault Ste. Marie
P6A 1Z7
(705) 759-1418

COCHRANE
Court House
Cochrane
P0L 1C0
(705) 272-4339

MANITOULIN
Court House
Gore Bay
P0P 1H0
(705) 282-2531

NIPISSING
Court House
North Bay
P1B 9L5
(705) 495-8305

PARRY SOUND
Court House
Parry Sound
P2A 1T7
(705) 746-4237

SUDBURY
Court House
Sudbury
P3C 1T9
(705) 671-5958

TEMISKAMING
Court House
Haileybury
P0J 1K0
(705) 672-3633

NORTHWEST REGION

REGIONAL SENIOR JUSTICE
The Hon. A. William Maloney
Court House
277 Camelot Street
Thunder Bay
P7A 4B3
(807) 475-1540

KENORA
Court House
Kenora
P9N 1S4
(807) 468-2831

RAINY RIVER
Court House
Fort Frances
P9A 1C9
(807) 274-5961

THUNDER BAY
Court House
Thunder Bay
P7A 4B3
(807) 475-1540

SOUTHWEST REGION

REGIONAL SENIOR JUSTICE
The Hon. B. Thomas Grainger
Court House
80 Dundas Street East
London
N6A 2P3
(519) 660-2291

ELGIN
Court House
St. Thomas
N5R 2P2
(519) 631-4810

ESSEX
Court House
Windsor
N9A 6V2
(519) 973-6630

HURON
Court House
Goderich
N7A 1M2
(519) 524-7581

KENT
Court House
Chatham
N7M 4K1
(519) 352-4040

LAMBTON
Court House
Sarnia
N7V 3C2
(519) 337-3265

MIDDLESEX
Court House
London
N6A 2P3
(519) 679-7020

OXFORD
Court House
Woodstock
N4S 4G6
(519) 537-5811

PERTH
Court House
Stratford
N5A 5S4
(519) 271-0750

DIVORCE ACT
(AND AMENDMENTS)

Divorce Act

R.S.C 1985, c. 3 (2nd Supp.)

[D-3.4]

An Act respecting divorce and corollary relief

*[1986, c. 4, assented to
13th February, 1986]*

SHORT TITLE

Short title

1. This Act may be cited as the *Divorce Act*.

INTERPRETATION

Definitions

2. (1) In this Act,

"appellate court" *«cour d'appel»*

"appellate court", in respect of an appeal from a court, means the court exercising appellate jurisdiction with respect to that appeal;

"child of the marriage" *«enfant à charge»*

"child of the marriage" means a child of two spouses or former spouses who, at the material time,
> (*a*) is under the age of sixteen years, or
> (*b*) is sixteen years of age or over and under their charge but unable, by reason of illness, disability or other cause, to withdraw from their charge or to obtain the necessaries of life;

"corollary relief proceeding" *«action en mesures accessoires»*

"corollary relief proceeding" means a proceeding in a court in which either or both former spouses seek a support order or a custody order or both such orders;

"court" *«tribunal»*

"court", in respect of a province, means
> (*a*) for the Province of Ontario, the Ontario Court (General Division),

(*a*.1) for the Province of Prince Edward Island or Newfoundland, the trial division of the Supreme Court of the Province,

(*b*) for the Province of Quebec, the Superior Court,

(*c*) for the Provinces of Nova Scotia and British Columbia, the Supreme Court of the Province,

(*d*) for the Province of New Brunswick, Manitoba, Saskatchewan or Alberta, the Court of Queen's Bench for the Province, and

(*e*) for the Yukon Territory or the Northwest Territories, the Supreme Court thereof,

and includes such other court in the province the judges of which are appointed by the Governor General as is designated by the Lieutenant Governor in Council of the province as a court for the purposes of this Act;

"custody" «*garde*»

"custody" includes care, upbringing and any other incident of custody;

"custody order" «*ordonnance de garde*»

"custody order" means an order made under subsection 16(1);

"divorce proceeding" «*action en divorce*»

"divorce proceeding" means a proceeding in a court in which either or both spouses seek a divorce alone or together with a support order or a custody order or both such orders;

"spouse" «*époux*»

"spouse" means either of a man or woman who are married to each other;

"support order" «*ordonnance alimentaire*»

"support order" means an order made under subsection 15(2);

"variation order" «*ordonnance modificative*»

"variation order" means an order made under subsection 17(1);

"variation proceeding" «*action en modification*»

"variation proceeding" means a proceeding in a court in which either or both former spouses seek a variation order.

Child of the marriage

(2) For the purposes of the definition "child of the marriage" in subsection (1), a child of two spouses or former spouses includes

(*a*) any child for whom they both stand in the place of parents; and

(*b*) any child of whom one is the parent and for whom the other stands in the place of a parent.

Term not restrictive

(3) The use of the term "application" to describe a proceeding under this Act in a court shall not be construed as limiting the name under which and the form and manner in which that proceeding may be taken in that court, and the name, manner and form of the proceeding in that court shall be such as is provided for by the rules regulating the practice and procedure in that court.

146

Idem

(4) The use in section 21.1 of the terms "affidavit" and "pleadings" to describe documents shall not be construed as limiting the name that may be used to refer to those documents in a court and the form of those documents, and the name and form of the documents shall be such as is provided for by the rules regulating the practice and procedure in that court.
R.S., 1985, c. 3 (2nd Supp.), s. 2, c. 27 (2nd Supp.), s. 10; 1990, c. 18, s. 1; 1992, c. 51, s. 46.

JURISDICTION

Jurisdiction in divorce proceedings

3. (1) A court in a province has jurisdiction to hear and determine a divorce proceeding if either spouse has been ordinarily resident in the province for at least one year immediately preceding the commencement of the proceeding.

Jurisdiction where two proceedings commenced on different days

(2) Where divorce proceedings between the same spouses are pending in two courts that would otherwise have jurisdiction under subsection (1) and were commenced on different days and the proceeding that was commenced first is not discontinued within thirty days after it was commenced, the court in which a divorce proceeding was commenced first has exclusive jurisdiction to hear and determine any divorce proceeding then pending between the spouses and the second divorce proceeding shall be deemed to be discontinued.

Jurisdiction where two proceedings commenced on same day

(3) Where divorce proceedings between the same spouses are pending in two courts that would otherwise have jurisdiction under subsection (1) and were commenced on the same day and neither proceeding is discontinued within thirty days after it was commenced, the Federal Court—Trial Division has exclusive jurisdiction to hear and determine any divorce proceeding then pending between the spouses and the divorce proceedings in those courts shall be transferred to the Federal Court—Trial Division on the direction of that Court.

Jurisdiction in corollary relief proceedings

4. (1) A court in a province has jurisdiction to hear and determine a corollary relief proceeding if

(a) either former spouse is ordinarily resident in the province at the commencement of the proceeding; or

(b) both former spouses accept the jurisdiction of the court.

Jurisdiction where two proceedings commenced on different days

(2) Where corollary relief proceedings between the same former spouses and in respect of the same matter are pending in two courts that would otherwise have jurisdiction under subsection (1) and were commenced on different days and the proceeding that was commenced first is not discontinued within thirty days after it was commenced, the court in which a corollary relief proceeding was commenced first has exclusive jurisdiction to hear and determine any corollary relief proceeding then pending between the former spouses in respect of that matter and the second corollary relief proceeding shall be deemed to be discontinued.

(3) Where proceedings between the same former spouses and in respect of the same matter are pending in two courts that would otherwise have jurisdiction under subsection (1) and were commenced on the same day and neither proceeding is discontinued within thirty days after it was commenced, the Federal Court—Trial Division has exclusive jurisdiction to hear and determine any corollary relief proceeding then pending between the former spouses in respect of that matter and the corollary relief proceedings in those courts shall be transferred to the Federal Court—Trial Division on the direction of that Court.

R.S., 1985, c. 3 (2nd Supp.), s. 4; 1993, c. 8, s. 1.

5. (1) A court in a province has jurisdiction to hear and determine a variation proceeding if

(*a*) either former spouse is ordinarily resident in the province at the commencement of the proceeding; or

(*b*) both former spouses accept the jurisdiction of the court.

(2) Where variation proceedings between the same former spouses and in respect of the same matter are pending in two courts that would otherwise have jurisdiction under subsection (1) and were commenced on different days and the proceeding that was commenced first is not discontinued within thirty days after it was commenced, the court in which a variation proceeding was commenced first has exclusive jurisdiction to hear and determine any variation proceeding then pending between the former spouses in respect of that matter and the second variation proceeding shall be deemed to be discontinued.

(3) Where variation proceedings between the same former spouses and in respect of the same matter are pending in two courts that would otherwise have jurisdiction under subsection (1) and were commenced on the same day and neither proceeding is discontinued within thirty days after it was commenced, the Federal Court—Trial Division has exclusive jurisdiction to hear and determine any variation proceeding then pending between the former spouses in respect of that matter and the variation proceedings in those courts shall be transferred to the Federal Court—Trial Division on the direction of that Court.

6. (1) Where an application for an order under section 16 is made in a divorce proceeding to a court in a province and is opposed and the child of the marriage in respect of whom the order is sought is most substantially connected with another province, the court may, on application by a spouse or on its own motion, transfer the divorce proceeding to a court in that other province.

(2) Where an application for an order under section 16 is made in a corollary relief proceeding to a court in a province and is opposed and the child of the marriage in respect of whom the order is sought is most substantially connected with another province, the court may, on application by a former spouse or on its own motion, transfer the corollary relief proceeding to a court in that other province.

(3) Where an application for a variation order in respect of a custody order is made in a variation proceeding to a court in a province and is opposed and the child of the marriage in respect of whom the variation order is sought is most substantially connected with another province, the court may, on application by a former spouse or on its own motion, transfer the variation proceeding to a court in that other province.

Exclusive jurisdiction

(4) Notwithstanding sections 3 to 5, a court in a province to which a proceeding is transferred under this section has exclusive jurisdiction to hear and determine the proceeding.

Exercise of jurisdiction by judge

7. The jurisdiction conferred on a court by this Act to grant a divorce shall be exercised only by a judge of the court without a jury.

DIVORCE

Divorce

8. (1) A court of competent jurisdiction may, on application by either or both spouses, grant a divorce to the spouse or spouses on the ground that there has been a breakdown of their marriage.

Breakdown of marriage

(2) Breakdown of a marriage is established only if

(*a*) the spouses have lived separate and apart for at least one year immediately preceding the determination of the divorce proceeding and were living separate and apart at the commencement of the proceeding; or

(*b*) the spouse against whom the divorce proceeding is brought has, since celebration of the marriage,

(i) committed adultery, or

(ii) treated the other spouse with physical or mental cruelty of such a kind as to render intolerable the continued cohabitation of the spouses.

Calculation of period of separation

(3) For the purposes of paragraph (2)(*a*),

(*a*) spouses shall be deemed to have lived separate and apart for any period during which they lived apart and either of them had the intention to live separate and apart from the other; and

(*b*) a period during which spouses have lived separate and apart shall not be considered to have been interrupted or terminated

(i) by reason only that either spouse has become incapable of forming or having an intention to continue to live separate and apart or of continuing to live separate and apart of the spouse's own volition, if it appears to the court that the separation would probably have continued if the spouse had not become so incapable, or

(ii) by reason only that the spouses have resumed cohabitation during a period of, or periods totalling, not more than ninety days with reconciliation as its primary purpose.

Duty of legal adviser

9. (1) It is the duty of every barrister, solicitor, lawyer or advocate who undertakes to act on behalf of a spouse in a divorce proceeding

(*a*) to draw to the attention of the spouse the provisions of this Act that have as their object the reconciliation of spouses, and

(*b*) to discuss with the spouse the possibility of the reconciliation of the spouses and to inform the spouse of the marriage counselling or guidance facilities known to him or her that might be able to assist the spouses to achieve a reconciliation,

unless the circumstances of the case are of such a nature that it would clearly not be appropriate to do so.

Idem

(2) It is the duty of every barrister, solicitor, lawyer or advocate who undertakes to act on behalf of a spouse in a divorce proceeding to discuss with the spouse the advisability of negotiating the matters that may be the subject of a support order or a custody order and to inform the spouse of the mediation facilities known to him or her that might be able to assist the spouses in negotiating those matters.

Certification

(3) Every document presented to a court by a barrister, solicitor, lawyer or advocate that formally commences a divorce proceeding shall contain a statement by him or her certifying that he or she has complied with this section.

Duty of court — reconciliation

10. (1) In a divorce proceeding, it is the duty of the court, before considering the evidence, to satisfy itself that there is no possibility of the reconciliation of the spouses, unless the circumstances of the case are of such a nature that it would clearly not be appropriate to do so.

Adjournment

(2) Where at any stage in a divorce proceeding it appears to the court from the nature of the case, the evidence or the attitude of either or both spouses that there is a possibility of the reconciliation of the spouses, the court shall

(*a*) adjourn the proceeding to afford the spouses an opportunity to achieve a reconciliation; and

(*b*) with the consent of the spouses or in the discretion of the court, nominate

(i) a person with experience or training in marriage counselling or guidance, or

(ii) in special circumstances, some other suitable person,

to assist the spouses to achieve a reconciliation.

Resumption

(3) Where fourteen days have elapsed from the date of any adjournment under subsection (2), the court shall resume the proceeding on the application of either or both spouses.

Nominee not competent or compellable

(4) No person nominated by a court under this section to assist spouses to achieve a

reconciliation is competent or compellable in any legal proceedings to disclose any admission or communication made to that person in his or her capacity as a nominee of the court for that purpose.

Evidence not admissible

(5) Evidence of anything said or of any admission or communication made in the course of assisting spouses to achieve a reconciliation is not admissible in any legal proceedings.

Duty of court — bars

11. (1) In a divorce proceeding, it is the duty of the court

(*a*) to satisfy itself that there has been no collusion in relation to the application for a divorce and to dismiss the application if it finds that there was collusion in presenting it;

(*b*) to satisfy itself that reasonable arrangements have been made for the support of any children of the marriage and, if such arrangements have not been made, to stay the granting of the divorce until such arrangements are made; and

(*c*) where a divorce is sought in circumstances described in paragraph 8(2)(*b*), to satisfy itself that there has been no condonation or connivance on the part of the spouse bringing the proceeding, and to dismiss the application for a divorce if that spouse has condoned or connived at the act or conduct complained of unless, in the opinion of the court, the public interest would be better served by granting the divorce.

Revival

(2) Any act or conduct that has been condoned is not capable of being revived so as to constitute a circumstance described in paragraph 8(2)(*b*).

Condonation

(3) For the purposes of this section, a continuation or resumption of cohabitation during a period of, or periods totalling, not more than ninety days with reconciliation as its primary purpose shall not be considered to constitute condonation.

Definition of "collusion"

(4) In this section, "collusion" means an agreement or conspiracy to which an applicant for a divorce is either directly or indirectly a party for the purpose of subverting the administration of justice, and includes any agreement, understanding or arrangement to fabricate or suppress evidence or to deceive the court, but does not include an agreement to the extent that it provides for separation between the parties, financial support, division of property or the custody of any child of the marriage.

Effective date generally

12. (1) Subject to this section, a divorce takes effect on the thirty-first day after the day on which the judgment granting the divorce is rendered.

Special circumstances

(2) Where, on or after rendering a judgment granting a divorce,

(*a*) the court is of the opinion that by reason of special circumstances the divorce should take effect earlier than the thirty-first day after the day on which the judgment is rendered, and (*b*) the spouses agree and undertake that no appeal from the judgment will be taken, or any appeal from the judgment that was taken has been abandoned,

the court may order that the divorce takes effect at such earlier time as it considers appropriate.

Effective date where appeal

(3) A divorce in respect of which an appeal is pending at the end of the period referred to in subsection (1), unless voided on appeal, takes effect on the expiration of the time fixed by law for instituting an appeal from the decision on that appeal or any subsequent appeal, if no appeal has been instituted within that time.

Certain extensions to be counted

(4) For the purposes of subsection (3), the time fixed by law for instituting an appeal from a decision on an appeal includes any extension thereof fixed pursuant to law before the expiration of that time or fixed thereafter on an application instituted before the expiration of that time.

No late extensions of time for appeal

(5) Notwithstanding any other law, the time fixed by law for instituting an appeal from a decision referred to in subsection (3) may not be extended after the expiration of that time, except on an application instituted before the expiration of that time.

Effective date where decision of Supreme Court of Canada

(6) A divorce in respect of which an appeal has been taken to the Supreme Court of Canada, unless voided on the appeal, takes effect on the day on which the judgment on the appeal is rendered.

Certificate of divorce

(7) Where a divorce takes effect in accordance with this section, a judge or officer of the court that rendered the judgment granting the divorce or, where that judgment has been appealed, of the appellate court that rendered the judgment on the final appeal, shall, on request, issue to any person a certificate that a divorce granted under this Act dissolved the marriage of the specified persons effective as of a specified date.

Conclusive proof

(8) A certificate referred to in subsection (7), or a certified copy thereof, is conclusive proof of the facts so certified without proof of the signature or authority of the person appearing to have signed the certificate.

Legal effect throughout Canada

13. On taking effect, a divorce granted under this Act has legal effect throughout Canada.

Marriage dissolved

14. On taking effect, a divorce granted under this Act dissolves the marriage of the spouses.

COROLLARY RELIEF

Definition of "spouse"

15. (1) In this section and section 16, "spouse" has the meaning assigned by subsection 2(1) and includes a former spouse.

(2) A court of competent jurisdiction may, on application by either or both spouses, make an order requiring one spouse to secure or pay, or to secure and pay, such lump sum or periodic sums, or such lump sum and periodic sums, as the court thinks reasonable for the support of

(*a*) the other spouse;

(*b*) any or all children of the marriage; or

(*c*) the other spouse and any or all children of the marriage.

(3) Where an application is made under subsection (2), the court may, on application by either or both spouses, make an interim order requiring one spouse to secure or pay, or to secure and pay, such lump sum or periodic sums, or such lump sum and periodic sums, as the court thinks reasonable for the support of

(*a*) the other spouse,

(*b*) any or all children of the marriage, or

(*c*) the other spouse and any or all children of the marriage,

pending determination of the application under subsection (2).

(4) The court may make an order under this section for a definite or indefinite period or until the happening of a specified event and may impose such other terms, conditions or restrictions in connection therewith as it thinks fit and just.

(5) In making an order under this section, the court shall take into consideration the condition, means, needs and other circumstances of each spouse and of any child of the marriage for whom support is sought, including

(*a*) the length of time the spouses cohabited;

(*b*) the functions performed by the spouse during cohabitation; and

(*c*) any order, agreement or arrangement relating to support of the spouse or child.

(6) In making an order under this section, the court shall not take into consideration any misconduct of a spouse in relation to the marriage.

(7) An order made under this section that provides for the support of a spouse should

(*a*) recognize any economic advantages or disadvantages to the spouses arising from the marriage or its breakdown;

(*b*) apportion between the spouses any financial consequences arising from the care of any child of the marriage over and above the obligation apportioned between the spouses pursuant to subsection (8);

(*c*) relieve any economic hardship of the spouses arising from the breakdown of the marriage; and

(*d*) in so far as practicable, promote the economic self-sufficiency of each spouse within a reasonable period of time.

Objectives of order for support of child

(8) An order made under this section that provides for the support of a child of the marriage should

(*a*) recognize that the spouses have a joint financial obligation to maintain the child; and

(*b*) apportion that obligation between the spouses according to their relative abilities to contribute to the performance of the obligation.

Assignment of order

(9) An order made under this section may be assigned to

(*a*) any minister of the Crown for Canada designated by the Governor in Council;

(*b*) any minister of the Crown for a province designated by the Lieutenant Governor in Council of the province;

(*c*) any member of the Council of the Yukon Territory designated by the Commissioner of the Yukon Territory; or

(*d*) any member of the Council of the Northwest Territories designated by the Commissioner of the Northwest Territories.

Order for custody

16. (1) A court of competent jurisdiction may, on application by either or both spouses or by any other person, make an order respecting the custody of or the access to, or the custody of and access to, any or all children of the marriage.

Interim order for custody

(2) Where an application is made under subsection (1), the court may, on application by either or both spouses or by any other person, make an interim order respecting the custody of or the access to, or the custody of and access to, any or all children of the marriage pending determination of the application under subsection (1).

Application by other person

(3) A person, other than a spouse, may not make an application under subsection (1) or (2) without leave of the court.

Joint custody or access

(4) The court may make an order under this section granting custody of, or access to, any or all children of the marriage to any one or more persons.

Access

(5) Unless the court orders otherwise, a spouse who is granted access to a child of the marriage has the right to make inquiries, and to be given information, as to the health, education and welfare of the child.

Terms and conditions

(6) The court may make an order under this section for a definite or indefinite period or until the happening of a specified event and may impose such other terms, conditions or restrictions in connection therewith as it thinks fit and just.

Order respecting change of residence

(7) Without limiting the generality of subsection (6), the court may include in an order under this section a term requiring any person who has custody of a child of the marriage and who intends to change the place of residence of that child to notify, at least thirty days before the change or within such other period before the change as the court may specify, any person who is granted access to that child of the change, the time at which the change will be made and the new place of residence of the child.

Factors

(8) In making an order under this section, the court shall take into consideration only the best interests of the child of the marriage as determined by reference to the condition, means, needs and other circumstances of the child.

Past conduct

(9) In making an order under this section, the court shall not take into consideration the past conduct of any person unless the conduct is relevant to the ability of that person to act as a parent of a child.

Maximum contact

(10) In making an order under this section, the court shall give effect to the principle that a child of the marriage should have as much contact with each spouse as is consistent with the best interests of the child and, for that purpose, shall take into consideration the willingness of the person for whom custody is sought to facilitate such contact.

Order for variation, rescission or suspension

17. (1) A court of competent jurisdiction may make an order varying, rescinding or suspending, prospectively or retroactively,

(a) a support order or any provision thereof on application by either or both former spouses; or

(b) a custody order or any provision thereof on application by either or both former spouses or by any other person.

Application by other person

(2) A person, other than a former spouse, may not make an application under paragraph (1)(b) without leave of the court.

Terms and conditions

(3) The court may include in a variation order any provision that under this Act could have been included in the order in respect of which the variation order is sought.

Factors for support order

(4) Before the court makes a variation order in respect of a support order, the court shall

satisfy itself that there has been a change in the condition, means, needs or other circumstances of either former spouse or of any child of the marriage for whom support is or was sought occurring since the making of the support order or the last variation order made in respect of that order, as the case may be, and, in making the variation order, the court shall take into consideration that change.

Factors for custody order

(5) Before the court makes a variation order in respect of a custody order, the court shall satisfy itself that there has been a change in the condition, means, needs or other circumstances of the child of the marriage occurring since the making of the custody order or the last variation order made in respect of that order, as the case may be, and, in making the variation order, the court shall take into consideration only the best interests of the child as determined by reference to that change.

Conduct

(6) In making a variation order, the court shall not take into consideration any conduct that under this Act could not have been considered in making the order in respect of which the variation order is sought.

Objectives of variation order varying order for support of former spouse

(7) A variation order varying a support order that provides for the support of a former spouse should

(*a*) recognize any economic advantages or disadvantages to the former spouses arising from the marriage or its breakdown;

(*b*) apportion between the former spouses any financial consequences arising from the care of any child of the marriage over and above the obligation apportioned between the former spouses pursuant to subsection (8);

(*c*) relieve any economic hardship of the former spouses arising from the breakdown of the marriage; and

(*d*) in so far as practicable, promote the economic self-sufficiency of each former spouse within a reasonable period of time.

Objectives of variation order varying order for support of child

(8) A variation order varying a support order that provides for the support of a child of the marriage should

(*a*) recognize that the former spouses have a joint financial obligation to maintain the child; and

(*b*) apportion that obligation between the former spouses according to their relative abilities to contribute to the performance of the obligation.

Maximum contact

(9) In making a variation order varying a custody order, the court shall give effect to the principle that a child of the marriage should have as much contact with each former spouse as is consistent with the best interests of the child and, for that purpose, where the variation order would grant custody of the child to a person who does not currently have custody, the court shall take into consideration the willingness of that person to facilitate such contact.

Limitation

(10) Notwithstanding subsection (1), where a support order provides for support for a definite period or until the happening of a specified event, a court may not, on an application instituted after the expiration of that period or the happening of that event, make a variation order for the purpose of resuming that support unless the court is satisfied that

(*a*) a variation order is necessary to relieve economic hardship arising from a change described in subsection (4) that is related to the marriage; and

(*b*) the changed circumstances, had they existed at the time of the making of the support order or the last variation order made in respect of that order, as the case may be, would likely have resulted in a different order.

Copy of order

(11) Where a court makes a variation order in respect of a support order or a custody order made by another court, it shall send a copy of the variation order, certified by a judge or officer of the court, to that other court.

Variation order by affidavit, etc.

17.1 Where both former spouses are ordinarily resident in different provinces, a court of competent jurisdiction may, in accordance with any applicable rules of the court, make a variation order pursuant to subsection 17(1) on the basis of the submissions of the former spouses, whether presented orally before the court or by means of affidavits or any means of telecommunication, if both former spouses consent thereto.

1993, c. 8, s. 2.

Definitions

18. (1) In this section and section 19,

"Attorney General" *«procureur général»*

"Attorney General", in respect of a province, means

(*a*) for the Yukon Territory, the member of the Council of the Yukon Territory designated by the Commissioner of the Yukon Territory,

(*b*) for the Northwest Territories, the member of the Council of the Northwest Territories designated by the Commissioner of the Northwest Territories, and

(*c*) for the other provinces, the Attorney General of the province,

and includes any person authorized in writing by the member or Attorney General to act for the member or Attorney General in the performance of a function under this section or section 19;

"provisional order" *«ordonnance conditionnelle»*

"provisional order" means an order made pursuant to subsection (2).

Provisional order

(2) Notwithstanding paragraph 5(1)(*a*) and subsection 17(1), where an application is made to a court in a province for a variation order in respect of a support order and

(*a*) the respondent in the application is ordinarily resident in another province and has not accepted the jurisdiction of the court, or both former spouses have not consented to the application of section 17.1 in respect of the matter, and (*b*) in the circumstances of the case, the court is satisfied that the issues can be adequately determined by proceeding under this section and section 19,

the court shall make a variation order with or without notice to and in the absence of the respondent, but such order is provisional only and has no legal effect until it is confirmed in a proceeding under section 19 and, where so confirmed, it has legal effect in accordance with the terms of the order confirming it.

Transmission

(3) Where a court in a province makes a provisional order, it shall send to the Attorney General for the province

(*a*) three copies of the provisional order certified by a judge or officer of the court;

(*b*) a certified or sworn document setting out or summarizing the evidence given to the court; and

(*c*) a statement giving any available information respecting the identification, location, income and assets of the respondent.

Idem

(4) On receipt of the documents referred to in subsection (3), the Attorney General shall send the documents to the Attorney General for the province in which the respondent is ordinarily resident.

Further evidence

(5) Where, during a proceeding under section 19, a court in a province remits the matter back for further evidence to the court that made the provisional order, the court that made the order shall, after giving notice to the applicant, receive further evidence.

Transmission

(6) Where evidence is received under subsection (5), the court that received the evidence shall forward to the court that remitted the matter back a certified or sworn document setting out or summarizing the evidence, together with such recommendations as the court that received the evidence considers appropriate.

R.S., 1985, c. 3 (2nd Supp.), s. 18; 1993, c. 8, s. 3.

Transmission

19. (1) On receipt of any documents sent pursuant to subsection 18(4), the Attorney General for the province in which the respondent is ordinarily resident shall send the documents to a court in the province.

Procedure

(2) Subject to subsection (3), where documents have been sent to a court pursuant to subsection (1), the court shall serve on the respondent a copy of the documents and a notice of a hearing respecting confirmation of the provisional order and shall proceed with the hearing, in the absence of the applicant, taking into consideration the certified or sworn document setting out or summarizing the evidence given to the court that made the provisional order.

Return to Attorney General

(3) Where documents have been sent to a court pursuant to subsection (1) and the respondent apparently is outside the province and is not likely to return, the court shall send the documents to the Attorney General for that province, together with any available information respecting the location and circumstances of the respondent.

Idem

(4) On receipt of any documents and information sent pursuant to subsection (3), the Attorney General shall send the documents and information to the Attorney General for the province of the court that made the provisional order.

Right of respondent

(5) In a proceeding under this section, the respondent may raise any matter that might have been raised before the court that made the provisional order.

Further evidence

(6) Where, in a proceeding under this section, the respondent satisfies the court that for the purpose of taking further evidence or for any other purpose it is necessary to remit the matter back to the court that made the provisional order, the court may so remit the matter and adjourn the proceeding for that purpose.

Order of confirmation or refusal

(7) At the conclusion of a proceeding under this section, the court shall make an order

(*a*) confirming the provisional order without variation;

(*b*) confirming the provisional order with variation; or

(*c*) refusing confirmation of the provisional order.

Further evidence

(8) The court, before making an order confirming the provisional order with variation or an order refusing confirmation of the provisional order, shall decide whether to remit the matter back for further evidence to the court that made the provisional order.

Interim order for support

(9) Where a court remits a matter pursuant to this section, the court may make an interim order requiring the respondent to secure or pay, or to secure and pay, such lump sum or periodic sums, or such lump sum and periodic sums, as the court thinks reasonable for the support of

(*a*) the applicant,

(*b*) any or all children of the marriage, or

(*c*) the applicant and any or all children of the marriage,

pending the making of an order under subsection (7).

Terms and conditions

(10) The court may make an order under subsection (9) for a definite or indefinite period or until the happening of a specified event and may impose such other terms, conditions or restrictions in connection therewith as it thinks fit and just.

Provisions applicable

(11) Subsections 17(4) and (6) to (8) apply, with such modifications as the circumstances require, in respect of an order made under subsection (9) as if it were a variation order referred to in those subsections.

(12) On making an order under subsection (7), the court in a province shall

(*a*) send a copy of the order, certified by a judge or officer of the court, to the Attorney General for that province, to the court that made the provisional order and, where that court is not the court that made the support order in respect of which the provisional order was made, to the court that made the support order;

(*b*) where an order is made confirming the provisional order with or without variation, file the order in the court; and

(*c*) where an order is made confirming the provisional order with variation or refusing confirmation of the provisional order, give written reasons to the Attorney General for that province and to the court that made the provisional order.

R.S., 1985, c. 3 (2nd Supp.), s. 19; 1993, c. 8, s. 4.

Definition of "court"

20. (1) In this section, "court", in respect of a province, has the meaning assigned by subsection 2(1) and includes such other court having jurisdiction in the province as is designated by the Lieutenant Governor in Council of the province as a court for the purposes of this section.

Legal effect throughout Canada

(2) Subject to subsection 18(2), an order made under section 15, 16 or 17 or subsection 19(9) has legal effect throughout Canada.

Enforcement

(3) An order that has legal effect throughout Canada pursuant to subsection (2) may be

(*a*) registered in any court in a province and enforced in like manner as an order of that court; or

(*b*) enforced in a province in any other manner provided for by the laws of that province.

APPEALS

Appeal to appellate court

21. (1) Subject to subsections (2) and (3), an appeal lies to the appellate court from any judgment or order, whether final or interim, rendered or made by a court under this Act.

Restriction on divorce appeals

(2) No appeal lies from a judgment granting a divorce on or after the day on which the divorce takes effect.

Restriction on order appeals

(3) No appeal lies from an order made under this Act more than thirty days after the day on which the order was made.

(4) An appellate court or a judge thereof may, on special grounds, either before or after the expiration of the time fixed by subsection (3) for instituting an appeal, by order extend that time.

(5) The appellate court may

(*a*) dismiss the appeal; or

(*b*) allow the appeal and

(i) render the judgment or make the order that ought to have been rendered or made, including such order or such further or other order as it deems just, or

(ii) order a new hearing where it deems it necessary to do so to correct a substantial wrong or miscarriage of justice.

(6) Except as otherwise provided by this Act or the rules or regulations, an appeal under this section shall be asserted, heard and decided according to the ordinary procedure governing appeals to the appellate court from the court rendering the judgment or making the order being appealed.

GENERAL

21.1 (1) In this section, "spouse" has the meaning assigned by subsection 2(1) and includes a former spouse.

(2) In any proceedings under this Act, a spouse (in this section referred to as the "deponent") may serve on the other spouse and file with the court an affidavit indicating

(*a*) that the other spouse is the spouse of the deponent;

(*b*) the date and place of the marriage, and the official character of the person who solemnized the marriage;

(*c*) the nature of any barriers to the remarriage of the deponent within the deponent's religion the removal of which is within the other spouse's control;

(*d*) where there are any barriers to the remarriage of the other spouse within the other spouse's religion the removal of which is within the deponent's control, that the deponent

(i) has removed those barriers, and the date and circumstances of that removal, or

(ii) has signified a willingness to remove those barriers, and the date and circumstances of that signification;

(*e*) that the deponent has, in writing, requested the other spouse to remove all of the barriers to the remarriage of the deponent within the deponent's religion the removal of which is within the other spouse's control;

(*f*) the date of the request described in paragraph (*e*); and

(*g*) that the other spouse, despite the request described in paragraph (*e*), has failed to remove all of the barriers referred to in that paragraph.

Powers of court where barriers not removed

(3) Where a spouse who has been served with an affidavit under subsection (2) does not

(*a*) within fifteen days after that affidavit is filed with the court or within such longer period as the court allows, serve on the deponent and file with the court an affidavit indicating that all of the barriers referred to in paragraph (2)(*e*) have been removed, and

(*b*) satisfy the court, in any additional manner that the court may require, that all of the barriers referred to in paragraph (2)(*e*) have been removed,

the court may, subject to any terms that the court considers appropriate,

(*c*) dismiss any application filed by that spouse under this Act, and

(*d*) strike out any other pleadings and affidavits filed by that spouse under this Act.

Special case

(4) Without limiting the generality of the court's discretion under subsection (3), the court may refuse to exercise its powers under paragraphs (3)(*c*) and (*d*) where a spouse who has been served with an affidavit under subsection (2)

(*a*) within fifteen days after that affidavit is filed with the court or within such longer period as the court allows, serves on the deponent and files with the court an affidavit indicating genuine grounds of a religious or conscientious nature for refusing to remove the barriers referred to in paragraph (2)(*e*); and

(*b*) satisfies the court, in any additional manner that the court may require, that the spouse has genuine grounds of a religious or conscientious nature for refusing to remove the barriers referred to in paragraph (2)(*e*).

Affidavits

(5) For the purposes of this section, an affidavit filed with the court by a spouse must, in order to be valid, indicate the date on which it was served on the other spouse.

Where section does not apply

(6) This section does not apply where the power to remove the barrier to religious remarriage lies with a religious body or official.

1990, c. 18, s. 2.

Recognition of foreign divorce

22. (1) A divorce granted, on or after the coming into force of this Act, pursuant to a law of a country or subdivision of a country other than Canada by a tribunal or other authority having jurisdiction to do so shall be recognized for all purposes of determining the marital status in Canada of any person, if either former spouse was ordinarily resident in that country or subdivision for at least one year immediately preceding the commencement of proceedings for the divorce.

Idem

(2) A divorce granted, after July 1, 1968, pursuant to a law of a country or subdivision of a country other than Canada by a tribunal or other authority having jurisdiction to do so, on the

basis of the domicile of the wife in that country or subdivision determined as if she were unmarried and, if she was a minor, as if she had attained the age of majority, shall be recognized for all purposes of determining the marital status in Canada of any person.

Other recognition rules preserved

(3) Nothing in this section abrogates or derogates from any other rule of law respecting the recognition of divorces granted otherwise than under this Act.

Provincial laws of evidence

23. (1) Subject to this or any other Act of Parliament, the laws of evidence of the province in which any proceedings under this Act are taken, including the laws of proof of service of any document, apply to such proceedings.

Presumption

(2) For the purposes of this section, where any proceedings are transferred to the Federal Court—Trial Division under subsection 3(3) or 5(3), the proceedings shall be deemed to have been taken in the province specified in the direction of the Court to be the province with which both spouses or former spouses, as the case may be, are or have been most substantially connected.

Proof of signature or office

24. A document offered in a proceeding under this Act that purports to be certified or sworn by a judge or an officer of a court shall, unless the contrary is proved, be proof of the appointment, signature or authority of the judge or officer and, in the case of a document purporting to be sworn, of the appointment, signature or authority of the person before whom the document purports to be sworn.

Definition of "competent authority"

25. (1) In this section, "competent authority", in respect of a court, or appellate court, in a province means the body, person or group of persons ordinarily competent under the laws of that province to make rules regulating the practice and procedure in that court.

Rules

(2) Subject to subsection (3), the competent authority may make rules applicable to any proceedings under this Act in a court, or appellate court, in a province, including, without limiting the generality of the foregoing, rules

(*a*) regulating the practice and procedure in the court, including the addition of persons as parties to the proceedings;

(*b*) respecting the conduct and disposition of any proceedings under this Act without an oral hearing;

(*b*.1) respecting the application of section 17.1 in respect of proceedings for a variation order;

(*c*) regulating the sittings of the court;

(*d*) respecting the fixing and awarding of costs;

(*e*) prescribing and regulating the duties of officers of the court;

(*f*) respecting the transfer of proceedings under this Act to or from the court; and (*g*) prescribing and regulating any other matter considered expedient to attain the ends of justice and carry into effect the purposes and provisions of this Act.

(3) The power to make rules for a court or appellate court conferred by subsection (2) on a competent authority shall be exercised in the like manner and subject to the like terms and conditions, if any, as the power to make rules for that court conferred on that authority by the laws of the province.

(4) Rules made pursuant to this section by a competent authority that is not a judicial or quasi-judicial body shall be deemed not to be statutory instruments within the meaning and for the purposes of the *Statutory Instruments Act*.

R.S., 1985, c. 3 (2nd Supp.), s. 25; 1993, c. 8, s. 5.

26. (1) The Governor in Council may make regulations for carrying the purposes and provisions of this Act into effect and, without limiting the generality of the foregoing, may make regulations

(*a*) respecting the establishment and operation of a central registry of divorce proceedings in Canada; and

(*b*) providing for uniformity in the rules made pursuant to section 25.

(2) Any regulations made pursuant to subsection (1) to provide for uniformity in the rules prevail over those rules.

27. (1) The Governor in Council may, by order, authorize the Minister of Justice to prescribe a fee to be paid by any person to whom a service is provided under this Act or the regulations.

(2) The Minister of Justice may, with the approval of the Governor in Council, enter into an agreement with the government of any province respecting the collection and remittance of any fees prescribed pursuant to subsection (1).

CONSEQUENTIAL AMENDMENTS

28. to 31. [Amendments]

TRANSITIONAL PROVISIONS

32. Proceedings may be commenced under this Act notwithstanding that the material facts or circumstances giving rise to the proceedings or to jurisdiction over the proceedings occurred wholly or partly before the day on which this Act comes into force.

33. Proceedings commenced under the *Divorce Act*, chapter D-8 of the Revised Statutes of Canada, 1970, before the day on which this Act comes into force and not finally disposed of before that day shall be dealt with and disposed of in accordance with that Act as it read immediately before that day, as though it had not been repealed.

Variation and enforcement of orders previously made

34. (1) Any order made under subsection 11(1) of the *Divorce Act*, chapter D-8 of the Revised Statutes of Canada, 1970, including any such order made pursuant to section 33 of this Act, and any order to the like effect made corollary to a decree of divorce granted in Canada before July 2, 1968 or granted on or after that day pursuant to subsection 22(2) of that Act may be varied, rescinded, suspended or enforced in accordance with sections 17 to 20, other than subsection 17(10), of this Act as if

(*a*) the order were a support order or custody order, as the case may require; and

(*b*) in subsections 17(4) and (5), the words "or the last order made under subsection 11(2) of the *Divorce Act*, chapter D-8 of the Revised Statutes of Canada, 1970, varying that order" were added immediately before the words "or the last variation order made in respect of that order"

Enforcement of orders previously made

(2) Any order made under section 10 of the *Divorce Act*, chapter D-8 of the Revised Statutes of Canada, 1970, including any such order made pursuant to section 33 of this Act, may be enforced in accordance with section 20 of this Act as if it were an order made under section 15 or 16 of this Act, as the case may require.

Assignment of orders previously made

(3) Any order for the maintenance of a spouse or child of the marriage made under section 10 or 11 of the *Divorce Act*, chapter D-8 of the Revised Statutes of Canada, 1970, including any such order made pursuant to section 33 of this Act, and any order to the like effect made corollary to a decree of divorce granted in Canada before July 2, 1968 or granted on or after that day pursuant to subsection 22(2) of that Act may be assigned to any person designated pursuant to subsection 15(9).

Procedural laws continued

35. The rules and regulations made under the *Divorce Act*, chapter D-8 of the Revised Statutes of Canada, 1970, and the provisions of any other law or of any rule, regulation or other instrument made thereunder respecting any matter in relation to which rules may be made under subsection 25(2) that were in force in Canada or any province immediately before the day on which this Act comes into force and that are not inconsistent with this Act continue in force as though made or enacted by or under this Act until they are repealed or altered by rules or regulations made under this Act or are, by virtue of the making of rules or regulations under this Act, rendered inconsistent with those rules or regulations.

COMMENCEMENT

Commencement

*36. This Act shall come into force on a day to be fixed by proclamation.

*[Note: Act in force June 1, 1986, *see* SI/86-70.]

RELATED PROVISIONS

—   **R.S., 1985, c. 27 (2nd Supp.), s. 11:**

Transitional: proceedings

"**11.** Proceedings to which any of the provisions amended by the schedule apply that were commenced before the coming into force of section 10 shall be continued in accordance with those amended provisions without any further formality."

—   **1990, c. 18, s. 3:**

Application of amendments

"**3.** Subsection 2(4) and section 21.1 of the *Divorce Act*, as enacted by this Act, apply in respect of proceedings commenced under the *Divorce Act* either before or after the coming into force of this Act."

—   **1992, c. 51, s. 67(1):**

Transitional: proceedings

67. (1) Every proceeding commenced before the coming into force of this subsection and in respect of which any provision amended by this Act applies shall be taken up and continued under and in conformity with that amended provision without any further formality.

—   **1992, c. 51, s. 68:**

Transitional: salary

68. (1) Notwithstanding the *Judges Act*, a person who holds the office of Chief Judge of the County Court of Nova Scotia immediately before the coming into force of section 6 shall continue to be paid the salary then annexed to that office until the salary annexed to the office of judge of the Supreme Court of Nova Scotia exceeds that salary, at which time that person shall be paid the salary annexed to the last-mentioned office.

Transitional: annuity

(2) Notwithstanding the *Judges Act*, the Chief Judge of the County Court of Nova Scotia shall, on the coming into force of this subsection, be deemed to have made an election in accordance with section 32 of that Act for the purposes of subsection 43(2) of that Act, and if, at the time of resignation, removal or attaining the age of retirement, is holding office as a puisne judge of the Supreme Court of Nova Scotia or the Nova Scotia Court of Appeal, the annuity payable under section 42 of that Act shall be an annuity equal to two thirds of the result obtained by subtracting five thousand dollars from the salary annexed at that time to the office of Chief Justice of the Supreme Court of Nova Scotia.

Idem

(3) Where, before the coming into force of this subsection, an annuity has been granted to or in respect of a judge of a county or district court of any province pursuant to sections 42, 43, 44 and 47 of the *Judges Act*, payment of that annuity shall continue in accordance with those sections, as they read immediately before the coming into force of this subsection.

—   1993, c. 8, ss. 19(1), (2):

Transitional

19. (1) Sections 4 and 17.1 and subsection 18(2) of the *Divorce Act*, as enacted by sections 1, 2 and 3, respectively, of this Act, apply only to corollary relief proceedings commenced under the *Divorce Act* after the coming into force of those sections.

Idem

(2) Subsections 19(2) and (7) of the *Divorce Act*, as enacted by section 4 of this Act, apply to corollary relief proceedings commenced under the *Divorce Act* before or after the coming into force of that section.

AMENDMENTS NOT IN FORCE

—   1993, c. 28, s. 78 (Sch. III, ss. 41 to 43):

41. Paragraph (*e*) of the definition "court" in subsection 2(1) is repealed and the following substituted therefor:

> (*e*) for the Yukon Territory, the Northwest Territories or Nunavut, the Supreme Court thereof,

42. Subsection 15(9) is amended by striking out the word "or" at the end of paragraph (*c*) thereof, by adding the word "or" at the end of paragraph (*d*) thereof and by adding thereto the following paragraph:

> (*e*) any member of the Executive Council of Nunavut designated by the Commissioner of Nunavut.

43. The definition "Attorney General" in subsection 18(1) is amended by striking out the word "and" at the end of paragraph (*b*) thereof and by adding thereto, immediately after paragraph (*b*) thereof, the following paragraph:

> (*b*.1) for Nunavut, the member of the Executive Council of Nunavut designated by the Commissioner of Nunavut, and

GLOSSARY

ADULTERY

Sexual intercourse with a person other than your spouse. For purposes of evidence, it is not necessary to have someone actually see the act.

AFFIDAVIT

A form of declaration made voluntarily, sworn before a lawyer or notary public and thus admissible in court as a statement of fact.

CERTIFICATE OF DIVORCE

Order that terminates the marriage and is irrevocable. It is granted after a waiting period of 31 days from the date of the Divorce Judgment.

CHAMBERS

It is best described as the private office of a judge where the only evidence allowed is affidavit evidence. There are no witnesses or juries, simply a judge who listens to applications, peruses the affidavit evidence, and grants (or refuses) orders based on this evidence. It is less formal than open court and because of this can be used only to obtain certain orders.

CHILD

Defined in section 2 of the Divorce Act and refers to any child under the age of 16 or over 16 but dependent on a parent because of illness, disability, or other cause.

CHILD OF THE MARRIAGE

A child of two spouses or former spouses who is under the age of 16 or 16 or over and under their charge but unable to withdraw from his or her dependency because of illness, disability, or other cause.

COLLUSION

An agreement between husband and wife that one of them shall commit, or appear to have committed, acts constituting a cause for divorce for the purpose of enabling the other to obtain a divorce.

COMMISSIONER

Person to whom is charged the administration of the legal process. All lawyers in Ontario are commissioners, but not all commissioners are lawyers. Commissioners must witness your signature to any and all affidavits.

CONDONATION

Forgiveness of any act or acts which are now being used as grounds for divorce. It means, in practical terms, that you continued to live with your spouse, or returned to live with your spouse, after learning of the act(s) in question.

CONNIVANCE

Active encouragement of your spouse's conduct by standing idly by and doing nothing about it could also be construed as a form of condonation.

COURT REGISTRY (Registrar's Office)

Place where all legal actions are processed. It is part of the machinery of the legal process. The employees are civil servants and not lawyers, but they are very knowledgeable in all phases of court proceedings and will help anyone who politely requests such help.

CRUELTY

Can be either mental or physical but must be of such a kind as to render intolerable the continued cohabitation of the parties. The test of cruelty is a personal one and can vary in the circumstances, i.e., what is cruel for one spouse may not be for another.

DIVORCE JUDGMENT

An order that you receive when you appear in court or once your documents have been processed. It is not the final order dissolving the marriage. A 31-day waiting period is required following the granting of the Divorce Judgment before you can obtain a Certificate of Divorce.

MOTION FOR JUDGMENT

This is a procedure by which you apply to a judge of the Ontario Court (General Division) for a Divorce Judgment. The Motion is made where the respondent is in default and has not filed an Answer within the prescribed time and requires a Requisition to the registrar and a Notice of Motion for Judgment. The Notice of Motion should set out the documentary evidence to be relied upon and should also set out whether you intend to present oral evidence at the hearing; otherwise the matter will proceed by way of Affidavit evidence.

NOTARY PUBLIC

Public officer whose function is to attest and certify certain documents and to perform other official acts. (**Note:** All lawyers are notaries public; not all notaries public are lawyers.)

NOTICE OF MOTION

Notice in writing to the other side stating that on a certain designated day at a specific place a motion will be made to the court for the purpose or relief stated in the Notice. A motion is different from a trial in that the procedure is more summary.

ONTARIO COURT
(Provincial Division)

The court that enforces applications made under the Children's Law Reform Act. It is located in various districts throughout the province.

PERSON NAMED IN THE PETITION

Person named in the petition (usually the co-adulterer) where no claim is made against that person for damages or costs.

PETITION

Written document containing an application by a person or persons and addressed to another person requesting the court to exercise its authority to redress some wrong or grant some privilege (e.g., divorce).

PETITIONER

Person who presents the petition to the court.

PLEADINGS

Formal allegations by the parties of their respective claims and defences submitted to the court for arbitration.

REQUISITION

Instructions to the registrar to take a certain step. In the usual case, to note the respondent in default. Such a step can be taken only when the Petition for Divorce has been filed with proof of service.

RESPONDENT AND CO-RESPONDENT

Person to whom the petition is addressed and usually defined as the opposing party. The co-respondent usually means the person charged with adultery with the respondent in a suit for divorce for that cause and joined as a defendant with such party if and only if some form of relief is claimed against the person. If no form of relief is claimed, the person may be named in the petition but is not a party to the action.

SUBSTITUTED SERVICE

Service upon a person in a manner other than by personal service. The method of serving substitutionally is authorized by statute, the most common being the publishing of notices in local newspapers in areas where they are most likely to be seen by the parties to whom the notices are addressed.

TITLE OF PROCEEDINGS

Title of the action including (in the case of divorce petitions) the court and registry numbers and the full names of the petitioner and the respondent.

TRIAL COHABITATION

An attempt by a couple that has separated to live together again. This does not affect the one-year separation period unless the period or periods of cohabitation total more than 90 days.

If you have enjoyed this book and would like to receive a free catalogue of all Self-Counsel titles, please write to:

Self-Counsel Press
1481 Charlotte Road
North Vancouver BC V7J 1H1

Or visit us on the World Wide Web at
http://www.self-counsel.com